Futureproofing Procurement

Futureproofing Procurement

The Importance of an Ethical and Sustainable Approach

Katie Jarvis-Grove

BEP
BUSINESS EXPERT PRESS
Leader in applied, concise business books

Futureproofing Procurement:
The Importance of an Ethical and Sustainable Approach

Cover design by Lynn Cobb & Charlene Kronstedt

Illustrations by Lynn Cobb

Interior design by Exeter Premedia Services Private Ltd., Chennai, India

First published in 2021 by
Business Expert Press, LLC
222 East 46th Street, New York, NY 10017
www.businessexpertpress.com

ISBN-13: 978-1-63742-054-6 (paperback)
ISBN-13: 978-1-63742-055-3 (e-book)

Business Expert Press Supply and Operations Management Collection

Collection ISSN: 2156-8189 (print)
Collection ISSN: 2156-8200 (electronic)

First edition: 2021

10 9 8 7 6 5 4 3 2 1

Description

This book demonstrates and explains how to best conduct yourself in a procurement role and what challenges you should be aware of. Factors such as being aware of modern slavery, supply chain's pollution emissions, and opportunities to recycle and reuse will be explored to create an understanding for the reader in how value should be achieved in today's way of managing procurement.

As you make your way through the book you will learn about tools and techniques that can aid you in making the right decision for you and your organization, to ensure that all ethical and sustainable elements of the procurement process are explored, evaluated, reviewed and documented.

This book discusses the ways in which procurement can help to provide an ethical and sustainable approach to business and product creation while raising an awareness of unacceptable practices with a view to their eradication.

You, the reader, will learn more about the authors honest experiences of working in procurement as you progress through her literary work. At the end of each chapter, she provides a mini case study exploring and explaining some of her purchasing stories that she has collated over the years.

Keywords

added value; benchmarking; bribery; child labor; collaboration; continuous improvement; corruption; cost; CSR; embezzlement; ethics; fraud; globalisation; human rights; mission statement; modern slavery; product life cycle; raw materials; recycling; social aspect; supply chain; sustainability; value stream mapping; vision statement

Contents

CHAPTER 1

An Introduction to Procurement and Its Evolution

What Is Procurement?

Procurement is a key function across industries. Regardless of sector, be it public, private, or third, procurement has an important role to play.

Public sector procurement is responsible for the spend of government-run organizations, and as such, has a large responsibility to manage that spend, which is the tax payers' money, with care and due diligence in accordance with strict policies and procedures.

Private sector procurement is responsible for managing the expenditure of a large variety of organizational spend, which includes everything from retail to insurance to manufacturing. Private sector procurement is not as stringently regulated as Public sector procurement, but this does not mean that procurement professionals should not exercise good practice.

Third sector procurement involves professionals investigating the best way to spend the money generated by donations, legacies, and fundraising. This sector is heavily regulated to make sure that funds that are being used are spent for the benefit of the cause for which they were given.

Sourcing, purchasing, and procurement are terms that are often and incorrectly used interchangeably, as they are considered to mean the same thing. They are not, and there is a distinct difference between the three functions.

Sourcing is the process that involves researching the market, seeking out and evaluating potential suppliers, and understanding the external or macro factors that may have an effect on the objective being met.

Purchasing is a transactional operation comprising the acquisition, ordering, and expediting of and payment for a tangible or intangible requirement. Purchasing can only happen once the sourcing process has been undertaken.

Procurement is the overriding term that encapsulates both sourcing and purchasing. Procurement is, or should be, a strategic function in all organizations to ensure value is added and money is saved. Procurement includes everything from the identification of a need from a stakeholder through to the payment and contract and supplier management.

Table 1.1 shows the clear differences involved in each of the aforementioned terms.

Sourcing and purchasing have a short-term objective focus, whereas procurement has a strategic, long-term focus and is related to organizational alignment.

From Table 1.1, it is clear to see that procurement involves a number of tasks and processes. These tasks and processes always follow the same order and should be followed if effective and value adding procurement is to be practiced.

Figure 1.1 shows the procurement process complete with all stages from 1 to 14 which are explained in Table 1.2 after the figure.

When procuring a *new buy*, the entire process is followed. This is because the product or service will not have been sourced before so every aspect has to be considered.

Table 1.1 Sourcing, purchasing, and procurement

Sourcing	Purchasing	Procurement
• Make-or-buy decision	• Obtaining a requisition	• Obtaining a requisition
• Specification development	• Raising purchase orders	• Make-or-buy decisions
• Market analysis	• Expediting orders	• Specification development
• Supplier identification	• Receiving orders	• Market analysis
• Supplier evaluation	• Checking order quality	• Stakeholder engagement
• Supplier selection	• Instructing payment	• Managing expenditure
		• Supplier selection
		• Raising, expediting, and receiving orders
		• Supplier engagement
		• Supplier management
		• Contract management
		• Compliance management
		• Corporate alignment

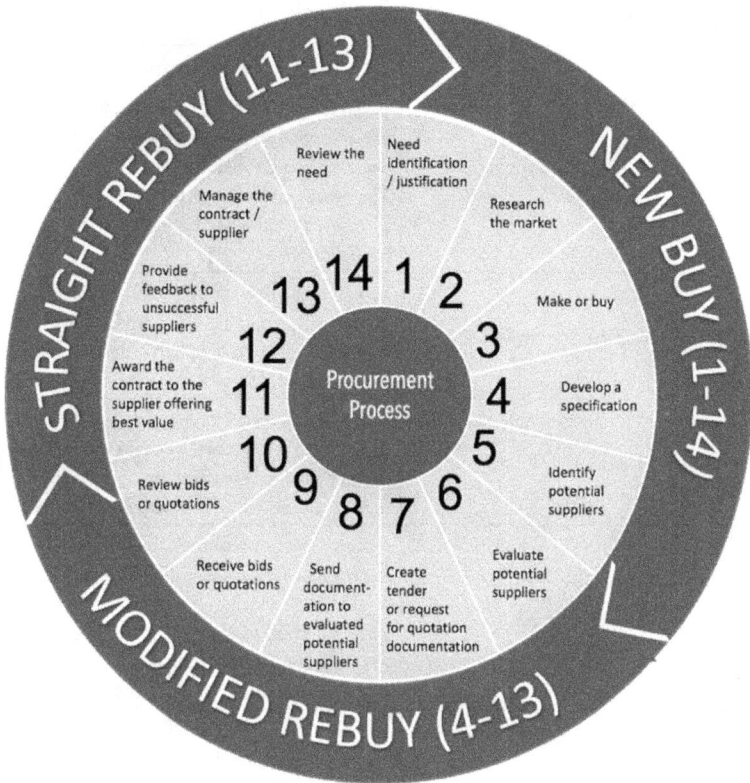

Figure 1.1 The procurement cycle

When working on a *modified rebuy*, only Stages 4 to 13 will be required. This is because the first four stages relate to preprocurement activity. A modified rebuy could be a slight amendment to a specification, a change to the quantity, quality or delivery details even the price.

If a procurement professional is seeking to carry out a *straight rebuy*, only Stages 11 to 13 are needed to be undertaken. This is because a straight rebuy is an identical process to the last. Nothing has changed between the buying organization and the supplier. The specification remains the same, but the quantity, quality, lead time, price, and delivery details are all unchanged.

The Evolution of Procurement

Procurement has not always been the function that we know in the 21st century. Like all processes, procurement has evolved over time, and as such, it has gained creditability as a value adding function to an organization.

Table 1.2 The procurement process explained

Stage	Term	Explanation
1	Need identification or justification	A stakeholder identifies the need for a product or service and advises the procurement department via a requisition. The procurement department conducts work to ensure that the need is justified and has been authorized.
2	Research the market	Research of the marketplace is undertaken. How readily available is the product or service? How many suppliers are there that can assist?
3	Make or buy	Evaluation is conducted to establish if the need would present best value to the organization by being brought in from an external supplier or created by the internal workforce.
4	Develop a specification	If the product or service is an *off-the-shelf* item, a specification may already exist. If the product or service is a new concept, procurement will need to work with the stakeholders to create and develop it. The specification may be conformance or performance.
5	Identify potential suppliers	Research is carried out to identify any suitable suppliers to fulfill the need. This could be through Internet searches, through procurement knowledge, via networking or recommendation.
6	Evaluate potential suppliers	The identified suppliers are evaluated based on factors such as financial stability, ethical conduct, capacity, and capability to fulfil the need and corporate compatibility.
7	Create tender or request for quotation documentation	An invitation to tender or a request for quotation is created including full details of the specification from Stage 4.
8	Send documentation to evaluated potential suppliers	Documentation is sent to all preapproved suppliers. This can be done via e-mail, an online portal, or by post. Ensure all suppliers receive exactly the same information to promote fairness and transparency.
9	Receive bids or quotations	The offers from the suppliers are returned via e-mail, through an online portal or by post.
10	Review bids or quotations	The bids or quotations are reviewed by procurement and possibly an award panel. To promote fairness, more than one individual should be involved in this process.

Table 1.2 (*Continued*)

Stage	Term	Explanation
11	Award contract to supplier offering best value	The contract is offered to the supplier who has offered the best value bid or quotation. The supplier is not obligated to accept so ensure that acceptance is gained prior to commencing Stage 12.
12	Provide feedback to unsuccessful suppliers	Contact is made with suppliers who have not been successful in gaining the contract. Feedback can be given to help the suppliers understand why they did not win the contract.
13	Manage the contract or supplier	The ongoing management of contractual performance and supplier relationships throughout the duration of the contract.
14	Review the need	The need may represent itself, in the same or a modified form—review it and start the process again.

In its infancy, procurement in the 1800s was purely transaction-driven. Somebody realized they needed something and that person or somebody else went and investigated that need. There was no planning or research, simply a reactional process to meeting an identified need.

Following on from this, in the late 1800s, people started to understand that planning made things easier and, procurement moved to being efficient and organized.

By the early to mid-1900s, the world had experienced two world wars, money was tight, and products were scarce. This produced the drive and motivation by procurement of saving money and parting with as little cash as possible.

As the end of the century drew closer, globalization was beginning to have an impact. No longer did procurement have to buy from local or national sources—it had become much easier because of transportation advances and technological development to make purchases from overseas. Procurement at this time was driven by international sourcing and saving money by working with less advanced economies. No concern at this point was given to any conditions or situations in which supplier found themselves.

At the end of the 1900s, procurement was realizing that the price of goods or services was not the sole factor to be considered. Cost was becoming apparent, and as this became better understood, procurement started to focus on being cost-driven-looking at ordering higher volumes to save money and considering that quality could be an important part of the supply chain.

Finally, today in the 2020s, procurement is thriving in its evolutionary journey. Now, procurement is a key function within forward-thinking organizations and forms part of the corporate strategy. This means that procurement is now heavily involved with aligning itself to mission and vision statements, working on organizational sustainability, and giving much thought to ethical and responsible sourcing for the benefit of the planet, the people, and ensuring a profit.

Figure 1.2 shows the evolution of procurement as an organizational function. In the 1800s, procurement was simply *reactive*. If a need was identified, the procurement process started there, and then with no preplanning, no supplier database or previous knowledge. There was little, if any, consideration for price, quality, or lead times—the need was identified and had to be met in whichever way it could. Toward the end of the 19th century, *efficiencies* were starting to be understood. Individuals conducting purchasing started to understand concepts such as buying in larger volumes and holding stock rather than being completely reactive. During the Second World War, when countries were trying to

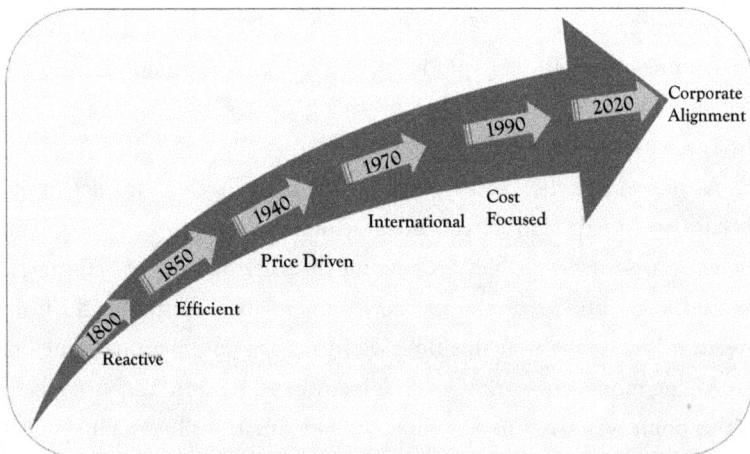

Figure 1.2 The evolution of procurement

manufacture items such as tanks, airplanes, and ammunition, and when money was tight, *price* became the most important factor. Individuals involved in purchasing were looking to secure goods and services at the lowest prices to allow higher volumes to be secured. After the war time had passed and the economies around the world started to develop, so did *international* trading. At this point of the procurement evolution, buyers started to look outside their local community for suppliers and started to engage with overseas organizations to fulfill the needs. The advancements in freight and transport aided this change, which allowed the start of importing more items from countries such as China. Buying from overseas opened up a new style of buying along with a larger variety of products, but in the 1990s, purchasing started to become procurement. All aspects of the sourcing process began to be considered. The quality, the lifecycle, and the lead time were understood to contribute toward the total *cost*. At this stage, procurement professionals started to evaluate quotations from suppliers based on more than just the price as they had historically and now realized that price, although important, was not the sole factor for comparing options. Now in 2020 and into the future, procurement is a function that considers all aspects and elements of not only the finished product or service but the contributing factors needed to acquire the goods. Areas such as environmental impact, sustainability, and aligning values with the suppliers are all taken into account along with price, lifecycle, quality, lead time, and volume.

Procurement Roles and Hierarchy

Procurement covers a vast array of processes, and as such, generates a multitude of roles that require fulfilling to ensure an effective function.

The most common roles in procurement are as follows:

Procurement Director

This role is the highest-ranking role within procurement. The person who undertakes this position has the ultimate responsibility for the procurement department, the strategy, policies and procedures, the spend management, compliance, and quality. This is a well-remunerated role, challenging yet rewarding, which requires an individual with a lot of industry experience and professional qualifications.

Procurement Manager

A procurement manager will report to the procurement director. While the procurement director role holds the highest level of responsibility, the procurement manager is involved in keeping the day-to-day operation running and ensures that the team is functioning effectively.

A procurement manager will have authority over senior buyers, giving him or her the final say in approving spend, signing off specifications, approving suppliers, signing contracts, and managing budgets. A senior buyer will be involved also in the day-to-day operations within the procurement department such as negotiation, supplier management, and reviewing key performance indicators or service-level agreements.

Senior Buyer

This role is filled by an individual who is well experienced. A senior buyer has a level of authority that is higher than buyers, and they are able to make some strategic decisions on behalf of the business. A senior buyer is likely to head up a team of buyers, junior buyers, apprentices, category managers, and analysts.

Category Manager

A category manager will be a specialist in the category they manage. Category managers are often present in larger organizations where there is a high level of spend across a significant number of categories. A category manager could, for example, be responsible for *direct* or *indirect* procurement of something more specialist such as *metals*.

Buyer

A buyer is a role that is quite generic in its title. A buyer can be responsible for an agreed amount of spend, a specific product or service, or an agreed department within an organization or procurement from one country. Buyers usually report to category managers in organizations that have a large procurement function.

Supply Chain Manager

A supply chain manager role is one that oversees the effective and efficient running of the supply chain, both upward and downward, from start to finish. A supply chain manager's responsibility is to guarantee safe delivery of goods and services to the consumer, mitigating against any risks that may be presented.

Supplier Relationship Manager

This role includes managing the relationships of current and potential suppliers to an organization through meetings, negotiations, and the monitoring and reporting of key performance indicators, service-level agreements, and general supplier performance. This role is likely to include a lot of time traveling to visit suppliers.

Procurement Data Analyst

A procurement data analyst role is one that involves gathering, collating, and interrogating data to provide team members with trends, forecasts, and predictions on what to order and when. The role also includes creating reports on suppliers based on their prices, quality performance, and delivery schedules.

Junior Buyer

A junior buyer role is a position that is carried out by an individual who is relatively inexperienced or new to procurement. This is a foundation level role in the building of a procurement career. A junior buyer will report to a buyer in a large organization.

Procurement Apprentice

Some countries operate government-funded or privately funded apprenticeships, which allows individuals coming directly from full-time education to enter a profession of their choice. A procurement apprentice role is suitable for somebody with no industry or procurement experience and who wishes to enter a career that involves working with the supply chain.

Expeditor

This role is based around the tracking of purchase orders from their placing to the point where the goods or services are delivered. An expeditor works closely with suppliers to ensure that the purchase orders are (1) received, (2) leave on time, and (3) arrive on time at the correct destination. An expeditor is an integral part of the supply chain who is responsible for advising on any delays or issues that may impact the procurement end to end process.

Materials Controller or Planner

A materials controller or planner role is one that ensures products are available as and when required while taking care not to hold too much inventory. This role involves the individual working closely with production and buyers to make sure that orders are placed in a timely manner to ensure stock levels are accurate at all times.

Warehouse Manager

While this role does not always fall within the procurement function, it is important to understand the part it plays within the supply chain. Warehouse managers' roles involve the assurance of stock being stored correctly and being available for transfer from a warehouse to the shop floor or to dispatch to satisfy customer and consumer needs.

Logistics Manager

This role involves the management of the movement of products and services throughout the supply chain. Logistics managers have to ensure that items are moved effectively throughout manufacturing plants, warehouses, and transport channels to reach their final destination in an acceptable form.

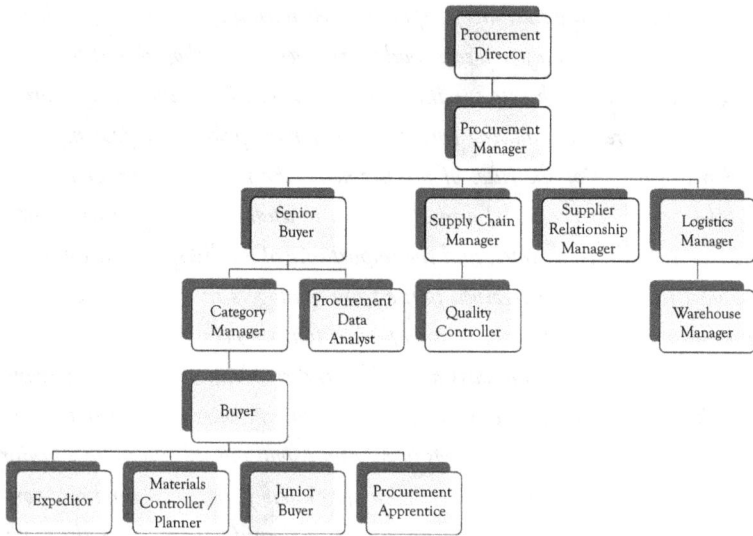

Figure 1.3 **Procurement department hierarchy**

Quality Controller

A quality controller is responsible for a product or service conforming to its specification. This may involve end product inspection, as well as working on the process that makes the product and identifying any way that improvement can be made to add value to the product.

Figure 1.3 shows the hierarchical structure of a typical procurement department. The diagram shows that the procurement director is in charge of the entire department, with the procurement manager reporting into them. The senior buyer, supply chain manager, supplier relationship manager, and logistics manager are all on the same tier and report directly to the procurement manager. The managers on tier three then have support staff working for them.

Author's Notes of Experience

During my 25 years in procurement, I have been lucky enough to have had many roles and experienced buying from a variety of industries, sectors, and organizations. My career started when I "fell" into buying. My official role in those days, the late 1990s, was an administrative assistant, but I was tasked with "sorting out the stationery cupboard." As with any project, I gave it my best shot, and within a few weeks, had rearranged the cupboard; put the pens, paper, and printer ink into specific and labeled locations; and set up reorder points to ensure that nothing ever ran out. I had spoken to a few suppliers and realized one of the rules of procurement (the more you buy or commit to take, the lower the price) and also began to understand the basics around price versus cost, lead times, and the importance of a solid specification. Over the next few months, I received praise from managers in the organization in two main areas. Firstly, they were impressed that they could always find what they wanted and it was always available, and secondly, the stationery spend was significantly below the predicted budget for the year. Due to that small project, a love of procurement was born, and I soon moved jobs to be a junior buyer for an agricultural company, then after a few years, sought more responsibility and got a job as a buyer for a kitchen manufacturer. Over the years, each job move gained me more responsibility, knowledge, and passion for the profession. In 2016, I had a role as a procurement manager for a large buying cooperative and had been in situ for nine years when I decided I wanted to give something back to the profession and share my years of experience. At that point, I left employment and set up my own business training people through delivering courses, writing books, and offering outsourced buying solutions. And, this is where I am now, in 2021, writing educational literature and delivering my own training material.

CHAPTER 2

Strategic Versus Transactional Procurement

Explanation of the Differences

In Chapter 1, it was explained that purchasing is transactional and procurement is strategic. So, what does this really mean, and what are the main differences between the two styles of obtaining goods and services?

In basic terms, the transactional process is one that is reactive and linked mainly to price and lead time, while strategic procurement includes all elements associated to the product or service, ensuring that the process is aligned with the organization to deliver or add value.

Value is not just obtaining the best price. Classically, value has been broken down into four areas:

1. Functional value
2. Monetary value
3. Social value
4. Psychological value

Value is more complex than this in procurement comprising many more factors which professionals should consider when exercising strategic processes.

Table 2.1 shows what constitutes value:

While value is a very important aspect of procurement, it is not always viable or a sensible use of resource, and therefore, it is good practice to evaluate the levels of value that can be justified in all purchases.

Figure 2.1 shows which products/services benefit from exploring the level of value that can be gained and that are not a good use of resource. A product or service that cannot be supplied by many suppliers and that

Table 2.1 Value

Value	Description
Aesthetics	The way a product looks can add value. A specification could be met, but it could be aesthetically unpleasing—this would not generate value.
Communication	Good communication adds value. Suppliers that talk or message their procurement colleagues generate value within the supply chain by sharing relevant information in a timely way.
Dependability	A supplier who is reliable helps a procurement professional to know that if they place an order within the agreement of a contract, the goods or services will be delivered. Dependability adds value by reducing concerns on failed delivery, poor customer satisfaction, and line stoppages within manufacturing.
Durability	Durable products add value. A product can be fit for purpose, can meet the specification but could also not be durable. If a supplier provides a durable product, this adds significant value to a procurement function.
Environmental awareness	Areas such as reducing emissions, lower pollution, recycling, using renewable energy, and removing plastic from the supply chain all relate to environmental awareness and can add value from a supplier to a buyer.
Ethical behavior	The supply chain should be ethical, free from slavery, and promoting equality and diversity. A supply chain that promotes ethical behavior will contribute toward value.
Innovation	A supplier who offers innovation in the supply chain can generate a lot of value. Innovative suppliers are likely to present themselves to relationships with strong communication and high levels of trust.
Lead time	Lead time being short for an urgent order would add value, while a long lead time for something that is a lower price would equally make the value more appealing.
Logistics	Effective logistical practice can add value by ensuring that products arrive where they should be within the supply chain at the expected time. Value adding in logistics also comes from reducing emissions, that is, choosing sea freight over air.
Packaging	Packaging that protects effectively, is made from renewable or sustainable sources, and that meets accredited standards adds value by reducing potential damage.
Price	Price will always be regarded as one of the most important factors within value. How much money an organization has to pay out is a key factor in all procurements and often holds the highest weighting within evaluation systems.

Table 2.1 (*Continued*)

Value	Description
Quality	The quality of a product or service contributes toward value. A fair price demands good quality. While it is illegal to supply anything that is not fit for purpose, this does not ensure that quality is always high, and therefore, quality must be measured to establish levels of value.
Relationships	Strong relationships add value as from these come dependability, innovation, and good communication.
Reputation	The reputation of a supplier has an impact on the procuring organization. Strong and positive reputations breed positivity, while a supplier with a poor or negative reputation may, by association, reduce the credibility of an organization.
Social aspects	A supplier who contributes to society in a positive way adds value. This could be through employing local residents, reducing pollution, or supporting a local community group.
Sustainable conduct	A supplier who is not sustainable will not add value. Sustainability relates to the longevity of the supplying organization, as well as the survival of the planet.
Transparency	Transparency adds value. If a supplier is open and honest about their policies, procedures, or potential problems, this promotes trust and in turn creates value.

has a high value to a business is known as *strategic*. These procurements are key to the organization functioning, and without them, the business would stop. Items that are available from only a few suppliers but have a low value are known as *inhibitors*. These products or services are also critical to an organization. While their financial value may be low, without these items, a product or service may not be able to be made or provided. Relationships between the buyer and the supplier should be collaborative when sourcing *strategic* and *inhibitor* category items. A *tactical* procurement is one where there are lots of suppliers, and the value is high. These products or services are readily available but cost a lot of money. The buyer would be in a strong position when sourcing a *tactical* item and would have more power than the supplier. The final quadrant is *transactional*. Here, items are readily available, there are a lot of suppliers to choose from, and they are low value. Relationships with suppliers are not important for these items, as buyers often swap their source of supply to achieve the lowest cost.

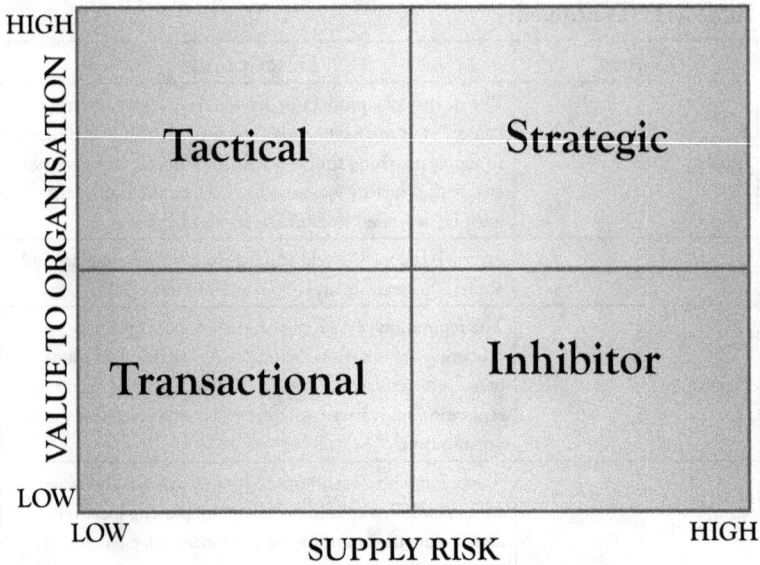

Figure 2.1 Product categorization

When Should Each Style Be Used?

As a procurement professional, most attention should be spent on strategic items. This is because the strategic products or services are directly linked to the core inputs or outputs of the organization, and as such, if these are not sourced effectively and with added value, the organization will not be long-term sustainable.

It is quite likely that the majority of an organization's spend is directly linked to strategic procurement.

To explain this logic, consider a vehicle manufacturing business. Strategic items to this organization will be the vehicle engines or bespoke bodywork. These are items that will have been developed with key suppliers and are integral to the end product being fit for purpose. If a procurement person did not spend the time and make the effort to ensure that these items were adding value to the organization, there is a high likelihood that the organization would start to lose profit and ultimately fail.

Opposing strategic products and services are transactional procurements. Using the same example, of a vehicle manufacturing company, transactional items could be products such as hand towels for the shop floor workers. While, ideally, procurement should ensure that these items are sourced as efficiently as possible, it is not a good use of time to spend several hours researching and negotiating over something that has a low spend and is available from multiple suppliers.

In between strategic and transactional, there are two other quadrants. Tactical items are products or services that have a high value to the organization with an abundance of suppliers in the marketplace. These products or services are tactical because a procurement professional can play the market, knowing that there will always be a supplier available to meet their needs. Here, money can be saved and value added by spending some resource on the products or services. Using our vehicle manufacturing example, a product could be a new company car for the CEO. Here, the procurement department is spending a lot of money but has many options to consider to get the best value outcome.

The final quadrant represents inhibitors. These products or services are items that are not available from many suppliers, but they are low value. In this situation, it would be sensible to work closely with and appreciate the suppliers. Here, the buyers need the suppliers more than vice versa, and if the supplier opted to no longer work with the procurement department, this could result in production stopping. For example, as per the previous description, with a vehicle manufacturing organization, products that could fall into this category could be a bespoke fastener that is required to hold in a key component. Without this fastener, the vehicle would not pass safety checks, albeit the fastener may only cost a few cents or pence.

Benefits of Strategic Procurement

The main outcome of strategic procurement is that an organization acquires products or services for an acceptable quality at a fair cost. Strategic procurement generates many benefits to an organization and the wider environment. Table 2.2 outlines some of the major benefits that an organization can achieve through strategic procurement.

As stated earlier in this chapter, the effort required to achieve collaborative relationships and practice strategic procurement is high, and therefore, a procurement professional has to be aware of what they are buying,

Table 2.2 Strategic benefits

Strategy	Benefit
Added value	All the elements of value from Table 2.3 are achievable through strategic procurement.
Enhanced relationships	Relationships will be more open, there will be a higher level of trust, and ideas will be shared through strategic procurement.
Environmentally friendly	Strategic procurement takes in to account futureproofing products, services, and solutions; therefore, the environment is taken seriously, and the least negative impact procurement can have the better.
Ethical good practice	Ethical concerns are addressed, managed, and mitigated against in strategic procurement—there is the long-term nature of procurement and relationships to consider and reducing bad practice across the globe is key.
Innovative solutions	Through strategic procurement comes collaboration, and collaboration breeds innovation—ideas for new and different ways of solving problems, meeting specifications, and reducing environment damage are encouraged and accepted openly.
Improved quality	Innovation enhances quality, and as such, improved quality is an outcome of strategic procurement.
Lean processes	Generating a reduction of waste in the supply chain is delivered from suppliers constantly trying to improve their offering, add value, and promote themselves as a leader in their field.
Lowest cost	Cost is reduced by all the elements in this table coming together to form a more sustainable and well-functioning product or service.
Risk mitigation	Suppliers who are in a collaborative relationship with procurement are keen to protect the business and the organization for which they work; therefore, risk will be mitigated against and managed carefully to try and avoid any unexpected problems within the supply chain.
Sustainable supply	Strategic procurement is about being able to rely on a supplier for a period of time, knowing that they will not run out of products, will remain financially stable, and will be socially acceptable.

how important it is to the organization, and the price to be able to make an informed decision if strategic procurement can be justified.

In an ideal world, all procurement would be strategic, but sadly, if that were the case, organizations would not survive. There will always be some products or services that require a transactional approach.

Risks of Transactional Procurement

As explained at the beginning of this chapter, there is a place for transactional procurement, but the strategy has to be well planned and thought through so that the risks associated with this style are minimized.

Transactional procurement works for items that are *routine*, items that are easy to source and that have a large supplier base. Transactional procurement is driven by price. Procurement professionals using transactional approaches will not spend time developing relationships with their suppliers, and as such, will not see the benefits detailed in Table 2.3.

The main risks associated with transactional procurement are shown in Table 2.3:

Table 2.3 Transactional risks

Transaction	Risks
Nonsustainable	Transactional procurement is not sustainable. Care for ethical practices, working conditions, and the planet are rarely considered.
Environmentally unfriendly	Environmental impacts are not considered, the main driver is price, and this is at the detriment to many factors, including the environment.
Relationship not valued	Relationships are often short term and not seen as integrative to any business strategy.
No loyalty	Suppliers are not likely to be loyal to their buyers, and buyers reciprocate this by disclosing prices or terms to the competition.
No innovation	Innovation is unlikely in transactional procurement. Buyers are expected to source what is available on the market, in its current form, and have no option to request changes.
High risk	As suppliers do not value the relationships highly, there is a high chance that they may change terms, cease production, or supply with little or no notice.
Supply chain failure	Transactional procurement increases the risk of not delivering the end product to the customer or consumer. As relationships are not collaborative and price is the main driver, suppliers may opt to supply the competition to the detriment of another buyer.
Price not cost driven	Transactional procurement is price driven—this means that sustainability, ethics, environmental awareness, loyalty, innovation, and reputation are not often taken into consideration. Price may save money in the short term, but cost delivers success in the long term.

Author's Notes of Experience

One of my roles throughout the years was working as a buyer for a cake manufacturing company. After my induction, I was tasked with reviewing the supplier relationships that my predecessor had formed and managed. To conduct this project, I knew that, first, I had to understand the importance of the products for which I was responsible so I created a Product Categorization grid based on the value of the products and their associated supply risk. Products for which I was responsible included flour, sugar, eggs, baking powder, ovens, packaging, and spare parts for the industrial mixers. Flour was placed in the top right quadrant of the matrix as there not many suppliers that could provide the exact specification needed, and the product was of critical importance to the business. Without flour, there would be no cakes. An example of a product that I placed in the tactical quadrant was the ovens. Having done some research it appeared that there were a lot of globally based suppliers of the industrial ovens that the business used, and therefore, I realized that I would have the opportunity to negotiate and see which suppliers could provide the best deal when it came to sourcing new ones. The paper cases in which the cakes the business made were placed prior to being put in their bespoke made boxes were only a couple of pence or cents each, and there was an abundance of suppliers. This product got placed in the transactional quadrant, as I did not think there was going to be any concerns getting the item with the volume of suppliers there was available. In the inhibitor quadrant, I placed the raising agent or baking powder that the company used. This was a low-value item, but very few suppliers, in fact, at that time, only two, were able to supply the quantities and specification that was needed.

Once all the products within my remit were categorized, I could review the relationships I had inherited and decide if the correct amount of attention was being given to each one.

I have to say that my predecessor did a good job, as the flour supplier relationship was collaborative, the oven suppliers were arms' length, and the paper case suppliers were transactional. The only fault I found was that the supplier of the raising agent was treated transactionally. That became the first change I made. I called a meeting with that supplier, introduced myself, and started to form a stronger allegiance. My company needed that supplier more than the supplier needed us. I was worried that without building a solid relationship, the supply of a critical ingredient to the cakes the organization baked could stop without any notice and cause significant problems. The supplier was receptive to the change in relationship, and during my two years in that role, I am proud to say that the company never ran out of raising agent and continued to supply quality, light, and airy cakes.

CHAPTER 3

Ethical and Sustainable Challenges

When working as a procurement professional and being involved in supply chains, it is important that knowledge is gained surrounding ethical and sustainable challenges.

Ethics form a significant part of everyone's lives and relate to the morals and accepted behaviors surrounding the ways in which activities are undertaken. Ethics reflect on what is good for individuals and what is tolerable within the society.

Figure 3.1 explores how ethics can be defined in relation to individuals' actions and mindsets. Positive behaviors such as transparency and honesty represent good ethical behavior.

Closely linked to ethics is sustainability. Sustainability is the ability to keep something at a constant level or rate. Sustainability is often referred to as linking to the environment, which is correct, but there are many other elements associated with sustainability when considering this subject in relation to procurement.

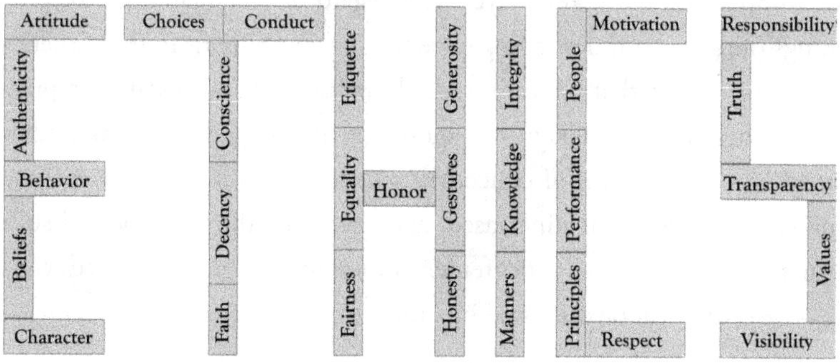

Figure 3.1 Elements of ethical behavior

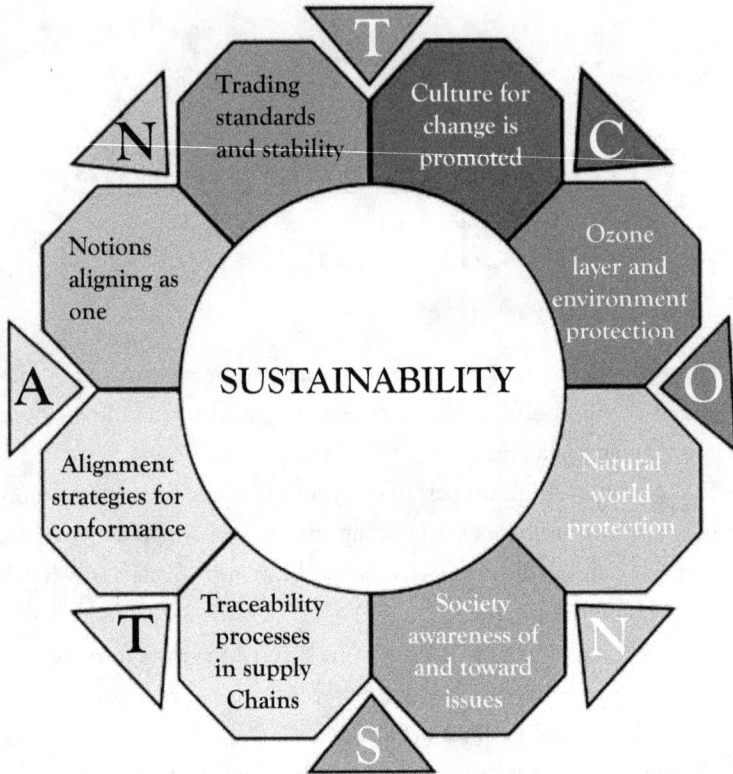

Figure 3.2 Elements of sustainability

Figure 3.2 shows what elements are associated with sustainability. The letters around the edge represent the first letter of the first word of each element, and when put together, spell *constant*. Things being constant is very important and a key player with regard to sustainability—keeping things the same, not destroying or removing anything from the planet.

To be certain that ethical standards are upheld and sustainable practice maintained, several key areas should be understood. When an understanding of these areas of concern is gained, the ability to manage and mitigate against them is increased, and therefore, the likelihood of such issues arising within the procurement function are significantly reduced.

Areas that will be discussed include:

- Modern slavery
- Child labor

- Working conditions
- Environmental challenges
- Product shortages

Modern Slavery

A common misconception is that it does not exist, as it was abolished in the 19th century. Slavery does still exist although the forms of slavery have changed. Modern slavery affects all countries across the world and continues to inflict harm on fellow human beings.

At the time of writing, circa December 2020, the estimated figures of individuals working in modern day slavery globally is 55 million.

Slavery in the 21st century is more about exploitation of humans rather than the *ownership* of an individual as was previously understood—regardless of the terminology, the stark fact remains that a large amount of people are being treated unfairly, and this could be present in any supply chain. Procurement professionals have a responsibility to be aware of all activities throughout the tiers of the supply chains they manage and seek to remove any unethical behavior from them.

Modern slavery comprises several different forms, including:

- Forced labor
- Bonded labor
- Descent-based slavery
- Human trafficking
- Domestic slavery

According to the International Labor Organization, forced labor is "all work of service which is exacted from any person under the threat of a penalty and for which the person has not offered himself or herself voluntarily."

Forced labor is thought to be the most common form of modern slavery across the world and is the most extreme form of the exploitation of humans. Forced labor is often targeted toward the most vulnerable groups of people within the world, groups such as discriminated against people. In many countries, women and children, and also migrants, are seen as the weaker beings, as these people can often be desperate for income, as well as having little or no understanding of the language spoken in the country in which they find themselves.

All industries and all sectors of the economy are susceptible to forced labor, and no organization is exempt. It is true to say, however, that some industries see a higher level of forced labor than others, and these include:

- Agriculture
- Construction
- Domestic work
- Manufacturing
- Sex work

Bonded labor occurs when a person agrees or is often tricked into working in return for paying off a debt. Bonded labor is most commonly seen in Southern Asia but can occur anywhere in the world.

Bonded labor is usually linked to several members of a family where all relations are found to be working toward paying off one member's debt. Inevitably, the debt never gets cleared, and families remain in a cycle of borrowing money from their employers to live and having to work continuously to pay off that ever increasing loan.

In some cases, bonded labor debts can be passed down the generations, so a child who has no awareness of where the debt originated from has to work to avoid getting beaten or abused in some way.

Bonded labor is rife in areas of high poverty, and industries such as agriculture and brick-making see very high levels of this type of modern slavery.

Descent-based slavery includes bonded labor situations where a child has to pick up a parent's role to continue to pay the loan back.

Descent-based slavery also relates to individuals who have been born into a lifestyle where their parents have been owned as slaves for generations before them.

This form of slavery is mainly found in areas of Africa such as Chad, Sudan, and Mali, where culturally, this is deemed an acceptable way of life. It is a sad fact that the women folk are often exposed to sexual assault and rape, which fuels the problem of bringing more children into this way of life.

The opportunities to escape from such a lifestyle are minimal. Children often do not have a birth certificate, an education, or an official identity, and therefore, many accept their fate and spend their lives in slavery.

Human trafficking involves the use of coercion to recruit people into a job where there is often no chance of leaving. Despite the word trafficking, this form of modern slavery does not mean that individuals have to be physically moved across borders or through countries—trafficking has evolved to mean introducing individuals to exploitative situations.

People can be trafficked into many jobs such as:

- Domestic slavery
- Drug dealing
- Forced marriage
- Prostitution

Domestic slavery is thought to involve an additional 67 million individuals in addition to the suggested numbers linked to modern slavery.

Domestic slavery involves individuals being exploited to work in private homes, conducting tasks such as cleaning, cooking, nannying, and doing laundry.

Individuals trapped within a cycle of domestic slavery may receive very low pay, or in some instances, no pay at all, but a basic accommodation in return for their work.

Domestic slavery really takes hold of an individual when their employer seizes their identity documentation such as passports and stops their contact with family members.

Child Labor

Child labor is best described as work that is done by minors, which deprives them of being children and that could have a negative effect on their development, be it physically or mentally.

Child labor is not illegal in all countries, but the general belief is that it should be eradicated. Organizations such as the International Labor Organization are championing the abolition of such practices and pushing for legislation to prohibit the existence of child labor.

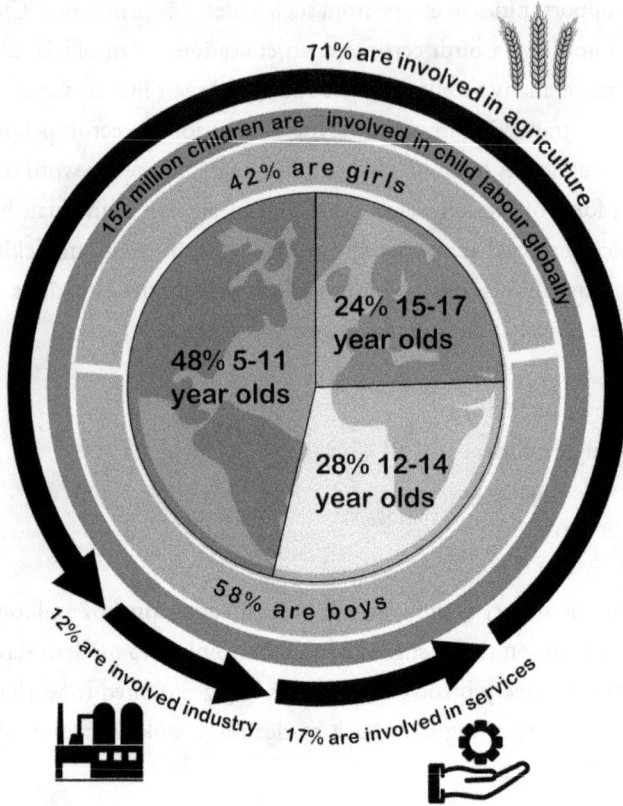

Figure 3.3 Child labor statistics

A sad fact is that globally, 152 million children are employed in child labor, and around half of those children are working in hazardous situations.

Figure 3.3 shows the statistics related to global child labor. The model shows how across the world, 58 percent of the child labor is boys and 42 percent girls, and then, it further breaks down the percentages of age groups of working children and the highest industry users of child labor.

Working Conditions

Working conditions relate to the environment in which individuals are expected to work and the way they are treated during that time.

Working conditions include the number of hours expected to be worked, in return for a fair remuneration, the amount of rest breaks to allow physical and mental recuperation, and other factors such as the temperature of working conditions, the availability of light, water, and fresh air. The supply of relevant protective clothing and machinery as well as training also falls into this category.

In today's society, it is expected that any worker is given a safe environment in which to work as well as having down time to experience a fair work–life balance.

Figure 3.4 shows what elements contribute toward working conditions. If an organization offers these elements, the working conditions will be favorable. For example, fair remuneration, regular breaks, and a good awareness of health and safety will contribute toward a happier environment in which to work.

The following case study shows how working conditions are still a concern in today's society.

In 2008, the female workers in supermarkets in Poland completed a survey. It was conducted as part of a wider project on. The main aim of the research was to identify and document the areas and forms of violation of employee rights in large retail chains.

Most of these workers were cashiers in the age range of 20 to 55 years.

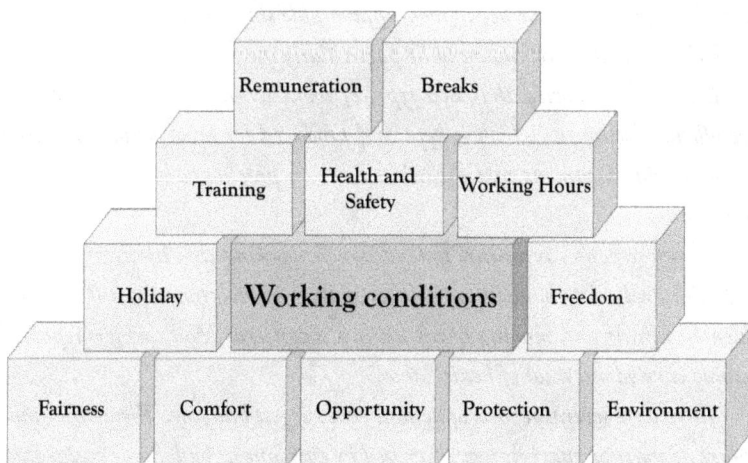

Figure 3.4 Working conditions

It is a fact that at least 80 percent of supermarket employees in Poland are female, and this is the group that was targeted for the survey.

The results of the survey generated some interesting information:

- *Long sequences of working days: Although each employee is enti-tled to 35 or more consecutive hours of rest in a week, in practice, rotas are frequently planned for seven or more continuous days. Extreme cases reported included 20 days of continuous work;*
- *The duration of shifts and time off: Weekday shifts last eight hours, and weekend or holiday shifts may be increased to 12 hours. An 11-hour break should be scheduled between the shifts. The research reported that workers are often expected to either work more hours or reduce the down time in between shifts;*
- *Difficulties in taking breaks during the day: During a duration of six hours of work, each worker is entitled to a 15-minute break. Employees reported that it is difficult to take breaks and were sometimes denied them. They indicated that may be linked to a staff shortage.*

The scheduling of shifts was another critical issue. Firstly, the schedules' different functions were uncovered. It was suggested that schedules were used as both a tool to plan and work the system, but also as a form of punishment. Staff members who had been absent or who had spoken up about their con-cerns were found to have been given unfavorable shifts and shift patterns and work days, which were known to be particularly busy.

It was also reported that two types of work schedules exist. One that is the official document, which is kept and produced for labor inspections, and the unofficial document that organizes work in practice, which staff have to conform to.

Survey responses indicated that although working conditions in relation to health and safety have improved, some areas of violation are still seen fre-quently. Lifting and moving heavy loads is a concern. Most cashiers reported having carried out a lot of heavy labor.

There were several reports of actions that suggest bullying. The work atmo-sphere at the supermarkets was described by everyone as bad. Some senior staff were reported to humiliate staff in front of other employees and customers or being generally disrespectful to them.

Although the findings of the research should not be generalized, they do suggest areas for concern in relation to the working conditions of female employees with supermarkets. The results also point to bottlenecks regarding the delivery of labor law. Breaches of working time appear to almost be commonplace.

While the findings appear concerning, it is only fair that more detailed research is carried out to assess further information on the claims.

Environmental Challenges

Procurement professionals face many environmental challenges in relation to the sourcing and supplying of products and services.

Challenges such as global warming, waste disposal, urban sprawl, and desertification, to name just a few, are situations of which procurement should be aware when creating contracts with suppliers.

Table 3.1 shows a more comprehensive list along with descriptions of the environmental factors of which procurement workers should be aware:

Table 3.1 Environmental factors

Challenge	Description
Acid rain	A corrosive downpour caused by the using of fossil fuels or spoiling vegetation
Air pollution	Fumes and waste gasses from vehicles and factories, which linger in the air
Climate change	The changing of seasons, the melting of icecaps, and rising of sea levels
Deforestation	The destruction of trees due to humans looking for new residential sites
Desertification	The process whereby previously fertile land becomes unfarmable due to drought or poor agricultural processes
Global warming	The vast use of greenhouse gasses, which has contributed toward the change in climate
Ground pollution	Contamination to the earth from landfill sites or the excessive use of chemicals
Light pollution	The excessive use of light, which can use additional energy and disturb the natural habitat of wildlife
Biodiversity loss	The extinction of animals, plants, or habitats
Noise pollution	Excess noise from industry or residential areas in previously unspoilt landscapes

Table 3.1 (*Continued*)

Challenge	Description
Ozone layer depletion	The reduction in the level of protective gasses surrounding the Earth due to the use of CFC gasses (a class of compounds of carbon, hydrogen, chlorine, and fluorine, typically gases used in refrigerants and aerosol propellants.) They are harmful to the ozone layer in the earth's atmosphere owing to the release of chlorine atoms on exposure to ultraviolet radiation
Urban sprawl	The spreading of residential areas from cities into areas that were once uninhabited
Waste disposal	The disposal of waste that is not recyclable that then contributes to land pollution
Water pollution	The disposal of waste into water courses or run off of chemicals from agricultural activity

Procurement has evolved to now be a function that should take in to account all elements of acquiring goods and services. An understanding of where products originate from, where they go, and how they are transported is key.

Procurement workers need to have an awareness of whether their chosen suppliers are working sustainably, that is, if a supplier is cutting down trees to supply timber, it is important that they have some form of regeneration program such as planting new trees.

The way that goods are moved around should be evaluated—air travel produces a significant amount of pollution, and as such, other less environmentally damaging options should be considered.

Factories manufacturing products, or organizations supplying services, should be reviewed to see whether they are making efforts to reduce their pollution levels and their carbon footprint. Procurement workers should engage with suppliers to work collaboratively on projects that promote sustainability. More information on this will follow.

Product Shortages

An additional challenge that procurement faces is that of shortages of products. As the impact of environmental and sustainability issues continues, the likelihood of a reduction in availability is almost guaranteed.

Raw materials such as coal, oil, and gas do not have an infinite supply, and as the amount available decreases, the prices will rise in accordance with the basic rules of supply and demand.

Figure 3.5 shows that if the quantity procured is low, the price is likely to be higher. The larger volume of a product or service that is procured, the lower the piece part price becomes. This is known as economies of scale. The point at which the quantity of products or services available equals the demand from procurement is known as equilibrium, and this is often where the best deals can be achieved. Equilibrium is the center point of the cross in the figure.

Procurement will be tasked with looking at securing volumes or investigating and sourcing alternatives without affecting the quality and the value of the products and services provided by their organization.

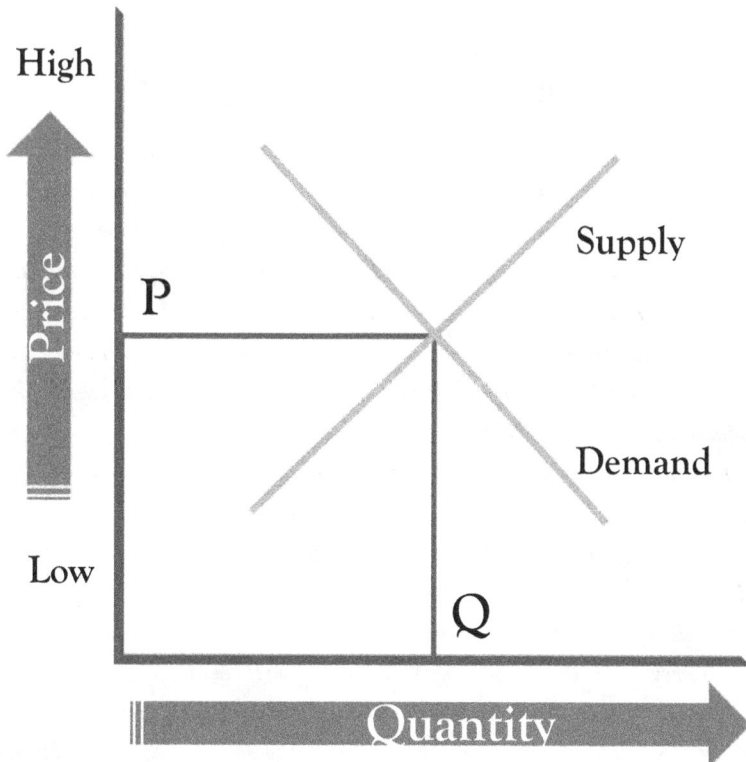

Figure 3.5 Supply, demand, and equilibrium

A rise in the population around the globe coupled with the constantly developing economic situation in emerging countries is expected to further increase the demand for food requirements in the future. The prediction is that by 2050, the global food requirement will have risen by 170%.

While this rise in demand is expected, it is neither known nor understood how the supply will be managed. Taking in to account the changes in climate and the evolving environmental concerns such as flooding and desertification, questions need to be answered as to how the level of food required will be able to be produced.

Some countries such as Japan have very low food self-sufficiency rates and will be under pressure to ensure supplies are secured to feed their people.

The future will undoubtedly present some challenges in the supply chain of global food and as such there is a need to look at the revision of food production in response to the ever changing economic and environmental situation in which the world currently finds itself.

Author's Notes of Experience

While working for a kitchen appliance manufacturer, I was lucky enough to go on a business trip to India to review the factories that were being used as outsourced suppliers to manufacture some internal parts for industrial ovens. The supplier was aware of the visit and was advised that myself and my assistant would be reviewing their processes and welfare policies. I will never forget what we saw in one factory in an Indian suburb. The first day's visit took place around lunch time and gave us no reason for concern. All the staff, which were woman, were busy working at their individual workstations, appeared to be happy and enjoying their work. The second day's inspection was a different story. We arrived on site at 0730, hours as had to catch a flight later that morning to go to a meeting with another supplier. As we walked into the same area of the factory as we had done the day before, we were astounded to see small children, probably no more than four years old, running around the machinery, while the women, later learned to me their mothers, were tidying up duvets, pillows, and blankets and putting them under their workstations behind the chairs on which they would later sit to do their day's work. Horrified, we enquired as to what the scene represented and were told calmly by the shift manager that these women and children live at the factory during the working week because their homes are about a three hour walk away, and it would not be practical for them to do two trips each day. Therefore, the business allowed the women and their children to sleep under their work benches for four nights a week, which guaranteed they would always be ready to start work at 0800 hours. During the hours that the women worked, the children were told to stay in a back room and "play." We were shocked and horrified at what we were discovering. Further questions gave answers explaining that the woman bought food for themselves and their one or two children with them when they arrived at the factory on a Monday morning, and that was their meals for the next few days.

Some of the women were happy to talk to us and explained that they did not mind living at work during the week, as it meant they were guaranteed to get money, which they needed to pay bills and keep their homes in the neighboring villages. Many of the women were widows and had no choice but to live this lifestyle if they and their children were to survive.

Myself and my assistant canceled our flight that we were due to take and rescheduled the meeting for the following day. We could not leave the factory knowing what welfare issues we had discovered. Several hours of discussions followed with the owner of the factory who, in fairness was a very nice man, and who thought he was simply helping women in need. We took the time to explain working and living conditions should not be in the same place, that the small amount of food the women and children had was not enough to sustain them, and that children should really not be left unattended for hours in a cold and damp room.

Despite the issues, the factory provided excellent products for the organization for which I worked, so the decision was made, once we returned to our office, to work with the supplier and educate them in working conditions, welfare, and health and safety.

As a procurement department, we learned a lot and realized that the extremely cost-effective solution we thought we had achieved was in fact far from that, and we were exploiting the Indian workforce. Over the following few weeks, the CEO of the organization worked closely with the Indian supplier to arrange living accommodation for the women and children that was offsite and for a tutor to be employed to educate the children. This of course had a knock-on effect on the price that we were paying for the goods but an increase that we happily absorbed and a lesson well learned.

CHAPTER 4

Reacting to Changing Consumer Needs

Consumer tastes, trends, and demands have always evolved and will always continue to do so. The nature of demographics is that people will move around, change their habits, and everyone will age—as such what people desire constantly changes.

However, in current times, the trend that is being seen across the globe is one linked to the consumer becoming more aware of what they are consuming. Price is not the sole driving factor and areas such as ethics, environmental awareness, and sustainability are being taking into account when money is being spent.

Figure 4.1 represents things that should be considered as well as the price when procuring. Elements such as any child labor or poor working conditions that may feature in the supply chain (ethics), the pollution caused through production of transportation, the drain on natural resources or damage to nature, the opportunities to recycle the product and/or its packaging at the end of its life, how sustainable the product is, and the reputation of the manufacturer or supplier should all be considered. Collectively, all these elements plus the price should be evaluated prior to making any decisions on which supplier to award an order to.

Consumers will now consider a range of factors before committing to make a purchase, and procurement professionals should be aware of this when sourcing raw materials, components, and end products to market.

Things that should be evaluated include:

- Country of origin
- Transport methods
- Environmental impact
- Ethical conduct in the supply chain
- Packaging

Figure 4.1 Considerations as well as price

- Percentage of recycled components
- Recyclability of end product
- Sustainable sources

Country of Origin

The country of origin is the country where the product or service was manufactured, produced, or grown. All products should display the country of origin so that consumers can see at a glance where their potential purchase stems from.

With such knowledge, consumers are now more likely to review the country of origin. Some consumers make a choice to buy from their home countries or continents where possible and where they can only select *homegrown* items.

Other consumers try to avoid countries where they know that child labor or modern slavery occurs or where there is little care for the environment.

Transport Methods

Associated with evaluating the country of origin is the consideration of the method of transport used to ship the goods. Some consumers are not in favor of products being air freighted across the world when there is an option to buy what has been grown or manufactured within their home country. This is particularly poignant in relation to fresh food such as vegetables, fruits, or meat. By encouraging the transportation of products from other countries and/or continents, the problems generated could include shortages of supply in the country of origin and the reduction of demand for homegrown items in the purchaser's own country.

The other side of the argument is that if a country that does not naturally have a climate to grow an item, that is, tomatoes in a cold climate such as Iceland, is it a better option to import them or use up all important fossil fuels to provide the heat and temperature that the plants need to thrive?

This is a challenging debate for which there is no correct answer, but it is something that procurement should be considering when sourcing. The key element for procurement to be successful is in meeting the true needs and demands of their stakeholders by understanding their demands, their beliefs, and their views.

The graph, Figure 4.2, shows a trend of the increased import of fruits and vegetables over the last few decades into America. As consumer demands push for a more local approach to sourcing needs, it will be interesting to see if this trend plateaus or the imports start to reduce as time goes on.

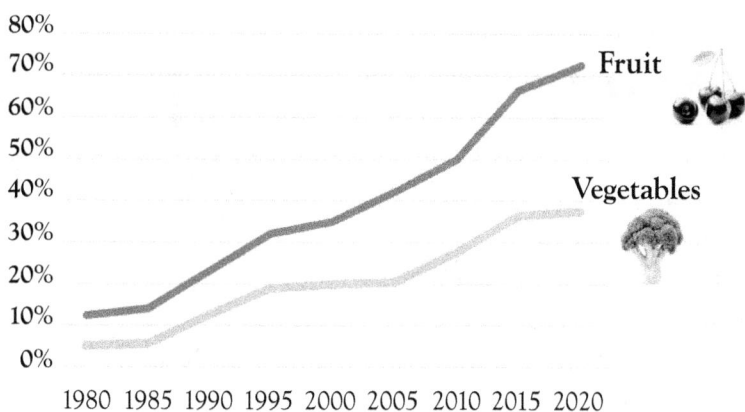

Figure 4.2 Fruit and vegetable importation trends

Environmental Impact

As explored in Chapter 3, there are a considerable number of environmental concerns and challenges that consumers are likely to take into account before making decisions on their purchase.

With the aid of technology, it is easier than ever before for customers and consumers to conduct independent research on the origin of products and any associated environmental problems that may be associated within the supply chain.

Understanding how raw materials are extracted, how components are manufactured, and how products are constructed is something that procurement professionals should make themselves aware of. Should a product be linked to a factory that is causing damage to the environment, this may provide a reason for a consumer to reject the finished goods.

Consider the fashion industry as an example—this is the world's second largest generator of pollution to the oil industry. As consumers learn about environmental damage that the fashion industry has caused and is still causing, there may be a shift away from well-known brands and market leaders. Procurement has an opportunity to proactively change the way that some industries function by working cross-functionally with designers and engineers to look at different options for sourcing materials and by engaging with suppliers who are keen to make positive changes in relation to the environmental impact.

One of the largest components in clothing is chemicals. Chemicals are used through the production of garments in processes such as bleaching and dyeing. This considerable use of chemicals, coupled with the intense growing and farming of cotton, is contributing heavily to environmental damage. It takes over 20,000 liters of water to grow 1 kg of cotton. While that volume of water is being swallowed up by cotton production, other waterways are being polluted with the waste chemicals that are being expelled from factories.

If procurement departments are able to engage with suppliers throughout the supply chain to work collaboratively and drive change, it is more likely that the consumer needs will be addressed, and customers will remain loyal to brands and organizations.

Ethical Conduct in the Supply Chain

As with the environmental impact, consumers are beginning to become equally aware of the ethical conduct within supply chains.

Consumers are taking the time to understand how their products are made, what processes are involved, and the effect this may have on people throughout the world.

Organizations such as Fair Trade, which is an internationally recognized global movement that promotes the importance of decent working conditions, local sustainability, acceptable terms of trade for growers, and better prices for all, are working tirelessly to try and meet the changing consumer needs. Products that are approved by such associations are able to display their logo, which demonstrates that the product requires the high standard required throughout the supply chain.

A globally known retail outlet axed several of its long-term suppliers based in India for their use of children in the supply chain.

The suppliers believed to be based in the area of Tamil Nadu were subcontracting the sewing of dresses to children working from their homes.

The retailer has grown to become one of the largest clothing stores in England with its discounted fashion. Some garments sell for around £1.

The vast majority of the products are sourced from low-cost countries, which is not a problem as long as ethical conduct is continuously monitored.

When confronted, the head of the store confirmed that they had sacked the suppliers in question due to their failings of acceptable ethical conduct, despite the fact that the supplier had been working with the organization since the 1960s.

The store had been conducting supplier audits, but the child labor elements of the supplier chain, through outsourcing, had not been picked up on until a whistleblower produced indisputable evidence, which forced action.

When the story broke, the media questioned the head of the store as to whether, if selling garments at very low prices, child labor was expected. The response stated by the head of the store was that child labor should not be part of any supply chain, and the way that this particular retail outlet was able to achieve the low resale prices was due to economies of scale and no expensive advertising campaigns.

The retailer was reported to be "very angry" with the findings, as they explained that they have tried hard to eradicate ethical misconduct through education and through audits.

The breach in ethical conduct was reported to the Ethical Trading Initiative where further investigation was carried out.

In a further act to manage and try to remove such instances from happening again, the retail outlet has reported to have engaged with a nongovernment-based organization in the low-cost countries to monitor and visit suppliers. This has been done with a view to try and detect any malpractice and eradicate it and the associated suppliers from the supply chain at the earliest possible opportunity.

Packaging

Consumers in some countries have been forced to visit their packaging habits. Some countries have banned the supply of plastic bags at checkouts, and others are charging a premium for shoppers to buy them. This is pushing consumers to bring their own reusable bags to try and reduce the environmental impact of disposal bags.

While in some areas, customer and consumers are being pushed to be more sustainable, many customers are making their own conscious decisions to review what they have purchased previously to see if it meets with their new or changed requirements.

Packaging is an area, which is changing rapidly—supermarkets are now considerably reducing the amount of plastic packaging on items such as fresh fruits and vegetables. Products are sold loose to aim to protect the environment.

In Europe, some supermarkets are aiming for a zero-waste approach, and packaging plays a major part in this vision—one privately owner supermarket in Germany has been successfully running a zero-waste enterprise for the last five years. The supermarket stocks a large variety of food and asks customers to bring their own containers into which they can put their purchases.

Fast-food outlets have reacted to customers' concerns about the amount of waste that they produce, and again, as per the supermarkets, several of the globally recognized outlets have looked to change the way they manufacture items such as straws and burger cartons, as well as making a concerted effort to place recycling points in eateries as well as more bins around areas where the restaurants are located.

Actions such as this are helping to protect business, as consumers are becoming more aware and demanding with what they expect from their supplier.

In the last 12 months, one of the world's largest online delivery companies has considerably reduced the amount of packaging used, standardized the sizes of cartons used, as well as taking the decision not to repack an item if the original equipment manufacturer (OEM) packaging is suitable to be used to further transport an item from the warehouse to the customers' address.

Without these reactive changes, businesses would start to see a decline in their sales and profit as customers' awareness of environmental impacts increases.

Percentage of Recycled Components

Changing consumer needs include the realization that organizations need to investigate the amount of raw materials being used in their products.

The supply of raw materials is not infinite, and as such, there is a growing trend to reuse materials as part of a more sustainable future.

Figure 4.3 outlines how products that were historically considered waste and disposed of can be reused and put back into the supply chain to promote sustainability.

It is part of the responsibility of procurement professionals to look at sourcing items that are not only manufactured from 100 percent raw materials but made up of a high element of reused or recycled products.

It is not uncommon to see items that are made from recycled plastic or recycled plastic, but the scope for reusing rather than disposing of items when they are no longer of use to the consumer is a lot vaster than is currently being exploited.

Ironically, one of the world's largest causes of pollution, transport, contains one of the most forward-thinking manufacturing processes in the aim to reuse others' waste.

Manufacturers such as Honda are now stating that they have a car for sale that is made from 90 percent recyclable parts, whereas Toyota has gone on record saying that 60 percent of one of their hybrid vehicle's

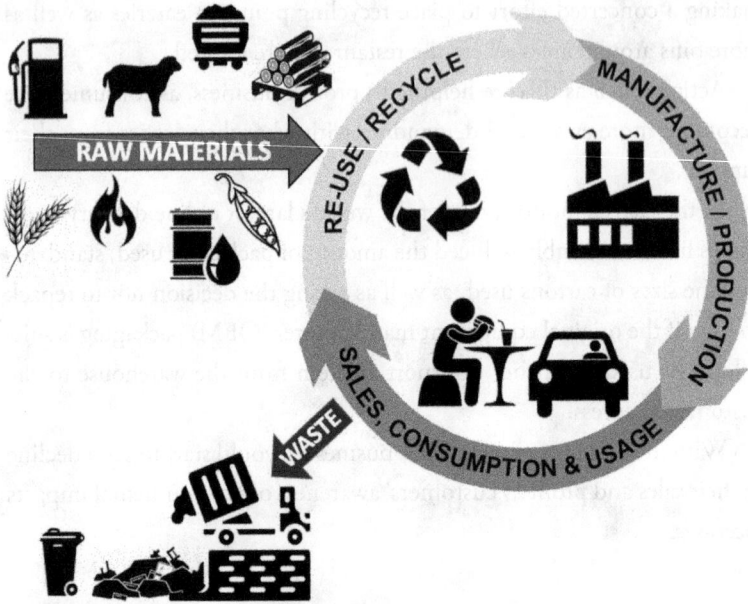

Figure 4.3 Sustainable production cycle

internal parts such as the seats, trims, and scuff plates are made from a *plastic* that has been grown from plants and is 100 percent eco-friendly.

Nissan has reported that their seats in one model are made from materials gathered from carbonated drinks bottles, and other recycled items have been used to make the dashboard and other traditionally plastic parts.

Recyclability of End Product

Customers and consumers are more aware than ever before about the importance of recycling products when they are no longer required. This could be items such as packaging but also things such as clothing, furniture, and cars.

Part of the decision process when purchasing an item is now linked to how recyclable the product is. Therefore, again for procurement professionals, it is critical when sourcing components, assemblies, or the finished products that this area is explored.

Many consumers want to help the environment: organizations have a duty of care to both the consumers and the environment, and as such, the sourcing of items, which will end up in a landfill, is not an acceptable practice if it can be avoided.

Sustainable Sources

While the end product is important to consumers as is the option to recycle or dispose of in a responsible manner, the way in which the product has come to exist is also something to be considered.

If a product is made using raw materials that are not being replenished, this is not deemed to be an ethical process. Suppliers or manufacturers that provide items requiring virgin materials such as timber should be replanting trees to replace what they are removing from the earth.

As well as the regeneration of raw materials, the wildlife and natural habitat linked to these virgin materials should be also protected. There is no excuse in the 21st century to destroy or remove something without replacing or replenishing supply.

In recent times, the media have reported on the unacceptable methods of growing and producing palm oil, which has been stated to have included burning down forests, causing significant pollution as well as destroying habitats where animals such as orangutans have lived for centuries.

Some leaders in sustainable food supply took the lead in late 2018 and stated that they would aim to remove all palm oil from their own brand items by the end of the year.

This was achieved, and one supermarket became the first to offer palm oil-free products to its consumers. This was done by reformulating over 100 products and introducing many hundreds of new or replacement items. It is estimated that approximately 450 products that had previously contained palm oil were now amended or replaced.

For consumers who are passionate about this particular ethical and sustainable subject, the supermarket retained and gained customers due to its action.

Finally, consumers are taking an interest in the resources used to manufacture or deliver their products and services. The use of renewable electricity is often explored to see how *green* a company is, as well as looking at the logistics of moving the products from place to place.

Global logistics companies are aware of what consumers, want and several are actively working toward and communicating the fact that they aim to produce zero emissions by the year 2050.

Procurement can contribute positively to all of the subjects mentioned in this chapter, and *how* this can be achieved will be discussed later in this book.

In the technological world in which most of the population now live, access to information has never been easier. As such, customers are more aware of what they are buying and how it came to be a product available for consumption.

Historically, consumers looked at a label, a brand, a list of ingredients, or if being very cautious, the country of origin to satisfy their concerns or curiosities of how a product had been created. In current times, that is not enough for most people.

Different lifestyle choices have created a larger number of vegans than ever before and a large number of environmentalists. These individuals are customers, and consumers demand the right to understand the full supply chain linked to their chosen product.

The Internet is the main tool by which this can be done, and as such, people are actively researching where products are sourced and looking for transparency in the supply chain.

Having this added awareness is forcing suppliers and manufacturers to act and become more sustainable if their wish is to continue being profitable into the future.

Procurement as a function plays a key role within this, as it is their role to source raw materials, components, and assemblies from the sources and suppliers that the general public finds acceptable.

This model outlines how the procurement organization works with three tiers of suppliers. The first tier is shown to be a local supplier, possibly in the same town or region as the buyer. Tier 2 could relate to the first regional supplier requesting part of their assembly to be manufactured in another country. The third tier may be that the global supplier has

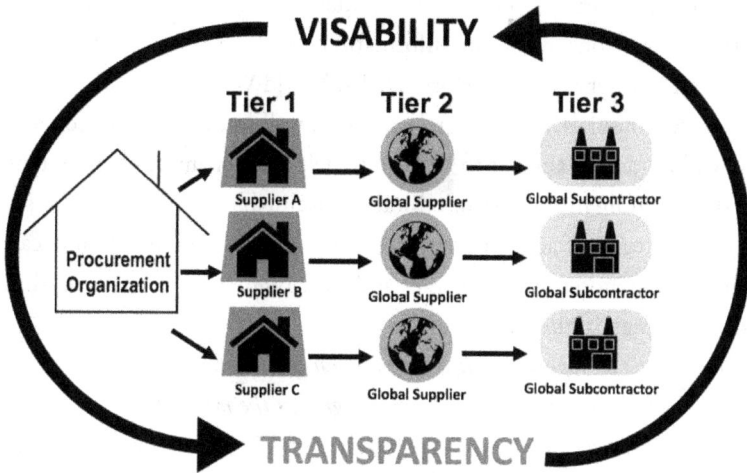

Figure 4.4 *Visibility and transparency*

outsourced part of their manufacturing process. Ultimately, if all tiers are transparent in their processes, the entire supplier chain has visibility, enabling the procurement organization able to see any poor practices or reasons for concern at the earliest opportunity.

Procurement workers have a duty of care to know exactly where the products they supply have derived from if true transparency throughout the supply chain it to be achieved.

Consumers are demonstrating a level of interest in sustainability in cloth-ing retail. Over 40 percent of people questioned said that they would be happy and willing to pay a higher price if it guaranteed them a sustainable garment.

Further feedback suggested that well over 80 percent of people would be open to purchasing clothes that were upcycled or recycled, and approximately 60 percent advised that they would cease to buy from a brand, should it be proven to have a negative effect on the environment.

The findings went on to show that despite only 20 percent of consumers actively looking to find sustainable options, if products had more informa-tion on them about where they came from, including any environmental impact that had occurred during the supply chain, more individuals would consider moving away from the cheaper options in favor of sustainable alternatives.

Gaining information on brand reputation follows a similar trend as to that of how consumers gain information on where products have come from and how services are performed. The World Wide Web holds details, stories, testimonials, and press releases from well-known and not so well-known brands and appears to be keen to help tarnish any companies that are doing wrong in the eyes of ethical or sustainable practice.

Being aware of just one negative story in relation to a brand can change the mindset of a consumer and steer them away from using that name or design in the future.

It was widely reported that a well-known global brand had a significant amount of breaches to labor and human rights in the mid-2010s.

The suspected violations were reported to be occurring across over 25 countries, and these included very poor working conditions, child labor, and unacceptable hours of work, with little amounts or no rest days, throughout the supply chain.

Reports also featured in the media regarding a small number of individuals taking their own lives while being forced to work in factories in Asia.

Other issues within globally leading organizations include the sourcing of materials for batteries for smart devices. The raw materials were revealed to have been sourced from unsustainable sources without responsible systems and processes in place.

The companies accused of such practices have been seen to attempt to improve their working practices. Programs have been reported to have been created to raise the awareness of health and safety in industry and to promote ethical and sustainable behavior.

Stories such as the aforementioned have been commonplace across the Internet and on social media. Whether proven to be factually correct or not, they still have a detrimental effect on brand reputation, and therefore, it is paramount for procurement professionals to ensure that the supply chain is understood, that all tiers are audited and any reasons for concern are raised and dealt with in a professional manner.

The use of market engagement in procurement is a good tool to try and understand what consumers want, how they want their products to look, where they want them to come from, and what environmental concerns they have. Positive use of market engagement is critical to developing

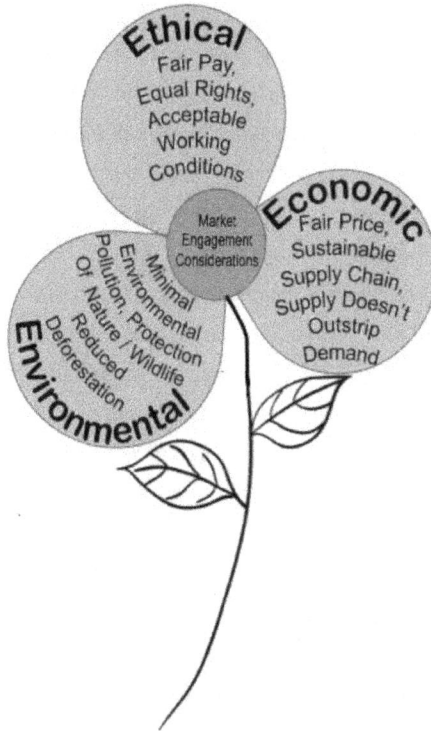

Figure 4.5 Market engagement factors

ethical and sustainable procurement and features from the outset an identified need as part of the specification creation and development.

Figure 4.5 shows what should be considered when engaging the market.

More information on the effective use of market engagement will feature in Chapter 6.

Author's Notes of Experience

In the mid-2000s I was part of a cross-functional project team created to try and reduce the amount of packaging being used in the distribution department of an agricultural spares company for which I worked. The company supplied wearing parts for tractors, combines, and lawnmowers, and parts ranged from a small nut or bolt right up to 200l drums of lubricants. At the start of the project, we established that the packaging department were using over 50 different sizes of boxes and had bubble wrap, shrink wrap, polystyrene, shredded paper, and air pockets to protect the shipments. Straight away it was realized that there was too much variety of packaging. The volume of boxes and associated products that were in the warehouse was staggering. We calculated if business remained static that there would be enough of over 50 percent of the items to last 10 years or more. This was due to the fact that the previous buyer had understood economies of scale and achieved low prices but had not appreciated that the demand was far less than the supplied amount.

Working with engineers, the cross-functional team deduced that the variation of packaging could be reduced by up to 70 percent. This meant that some products would be dispatched in larger boxes than was necessary, but this gave the company the opportunity to use up some of the surplus protective items such as bubble wrap.

Over the course of 18 months, the stock slowly depleted to a level where we could look at sourcing new sizes and more appropriate methods of packaging. The main changes that the team made were to invest in a cardboard chipper so that any boxes that were received at goods in were broken down and made into small pieces, which were then used to protect items leaving the company. This ticked the box for recycling and reusing rather than generating waste. The company also invested in returnable stillages so that the regular customers who took large or high volumes of items on a regular basis got two crates assigned to them. When one crate of goods was delivered, the courier was instructed to collect the crate from the last delivery and return it to our company.

When I left that company, the area in the warehouse that was once full to bursting with boxes, plastic, and other packaging items was being renovated to house more strategic and fast-moving stock items. Due to the reduction in packing, which created more space and the cost saved in not procuring so much, the organization was able to justify holding more inventory with a view to expanding. The company is still going from strength to strength 15 years later, and I believe that the cardboard chipper is still in situ and the crate system, albeit refreshed crates, is still proving effective.

CHAPTER 5

Price Versus Cost: Supplier Evaluation and Relationship Management

One of the first and most important rules of ensuring ethical and sustainable procurement is understanding the fundamental difference between price and cost.

Both price and cost are terms that are used interchangeably, often without understanding the differences between them.

Figure 5.1 shows visually the differences between the two. Price is simply the amount of money exchanged in return for goods or services. Cost includes the insurance, lead time, ethics, and potential fluctuation of currency as well as other factors that should be evaluated.

Price is the amount of money a person parts with to secure their purchase. Nothing else is included in the price element of a procurement.

Figure 5.1 Price versus cost

Cost, however, is much more in depth. Cost includes many factors, which are explained in Table 5.1.

Table 5.1 Cost factors

Element of cost	Things to consider
Quality	Is the product/service of a high or low quality?
Disposal	Can the product or by-products from a service be disposed of easily and in an environmentally friendly manner?
Lead time	How long does it take to receive the procurement after the purchase order has been placed?
Cycle time	How long does the product take to be manufactured?
Reputation	Does the supplier or distributor have a good reputation?
Ethical concerns	Is the supply chain that links to the product or service free of child labor, bribery, corruption, and positively working to promote good conditions and fair pay?
Sustainability	Is the supply chain that relates to the product of service sustainable in both an environmental and economic way?
Maintenance	Does the product require a high level of maintenance? Is this included in the price, or is it extra?
Servicing	Does the product require servicing? If so, how often, and how much is the price? Cost for this?
Warranty	Does the product or service come with a warranty to ensure the consumers' satisfaction? Is this free or an additional charge?
Guarantee	What length of guarantee comes with the procurement?
Currency fluctuation	If buying in foreign tender, what is the exchange rate? Is it fixed for the procurement, or is there a risk associated with it?
Durability	How structurally sound is the procurement? Will it last a long time or break down during use?
Fit for purpose	Is the product or service fit for purpose? Does it do what is needed to adequately fulfil the need?
Price	How much money will have to be exchanged in return for the product or service?
Delivery	Is delivery included in the price, or could this be an additional amount for consideration?
Insurance	Does the supplier provide insurance for the product or service while it is being transported or provide?
INCO terms	What INCO terms have been agreed? Who is responsible for the cost of transport, duties, taxes, and insurance?
Brand	Is the brand a well-known and accepted one, which would add value, or is it unknown or poorly adopted?
Recyclability	Can the product or tangible items linked to the service be recycled? If not, what effect would this have on the environment?

Evaluation

When evaluating a supplier to establish if they are a suitable match to work with a procurement function's organization, all the factors featured in Table 5.1 have to be explored, as well as checks on the proposed suppliers.

If a supplier is able to provide a quotation that appears to be a good overall cost, procurement workers then have to be certain that the supplier is a sustainable choice for contract award.

While the cost may appear fair, if the supplier is not going to be able to fulfil their contractual obligations, this would be a reason for concern.

Table 5.2 shows a list of some of the areas that a procurement worker should investigate and evaluate prior to awarding a contract.

While the factors stated in Tables 5.1 and 5.2 are always important areas for consideration, more time should be spent on this evaluation for procurements that are strategic or critical to an organization.

In an ideal world where time is limitless and resources are open-ended, it would be good practice to conduct a thorough evaluation on every

Table 5.2 Investigation and evaluation criteria

Check for	Description
Regulation	Is the supplier adhering to industry rules and processes to ensure that goods or services conform?
Capacity	Does the supplier have the space, machinery, and resources needed within their operation to fulfil the potential orders?
Competence	While the supplier may have the machinery, technology, or required capacity, do they have the knowledge and skills to fulfil the contract?
Standards	What standards does the supplier work to? Are they in possession of a globally recognized standard such as ISO9001 for quality or ISO14001 for environmental conduct?
Finance	Is the supplier cash-rich? Do they have a good cash flow? Are they liquid? Are they highly geared? A supplier must have access to cash in order to buy raw materials throughout the contract duration.
Technology	Is the technology used within the procurement organization compatible with that of the suppliers' business? Can the machinery talk to each other if needed?
Alignment	Are the two organizations aligned? Do they share a similar vision, working methods, and cultural values?
Dedication	Is the supplier going to be loyal and work collaboratively with the buying organization? A supplier needs to be committed to providing continuous supply throughout the contractual term.

supplier for every item sourced. This, however, is not practical and would lead to organizations having to charge prices that were not in keeping with the market and then, ironically, the organization would not be sustainable.

While the mindset is in the process of being changed to be made more aware of ethics and sustainability, the focus needs to be on the big spend items, the products, and services without which an organization would not function.

Products and services fall into four categories within procurement, as originally explained in Figure 2.1.

As a reminder, products or services in the strategic category are procurements where there is a high amount of money spent on that item, but there are limited supplier options. This could be that the product or service is a specialist item, that the supplier is a monopoly, or that there is not a lot of demand for the item apart from a couple of organizations.

Inhibitor items are of high importance to an organization—without them, the end products or services would not be able to be manufactured or provided. Bottleneck products are not expensive, but there is not a lot of supplier choice.

Tactical items are products or services that are of high value and where there are a lot of suppliers from which to choose. These items tend to be capital purchases (CAPEX) such as machinery or vehicles.

Finally, the items that are of low value and where there are a lot of suppliers to choose from are known as noncritical or transactional. These items are readily available, and buyers often find themselves in a situation of perfect competition when sourcing these. The importance of understanding the different types of product category is related to the way in which suppliers are seen by the procurement function. For example, a supplier of a transactional product or service would not require as much evaluation or management as a supplier of a core component (strategic) or a manufacturing process.

Styles of Relationships

Relationships vary considerably within procurement between buyers and suppliers, and this is demonstrated in Figure 5.2. The axis on the model ranges from low to high and shows the level of trust, commitment ,and communication increasing as the style of relationship improves.

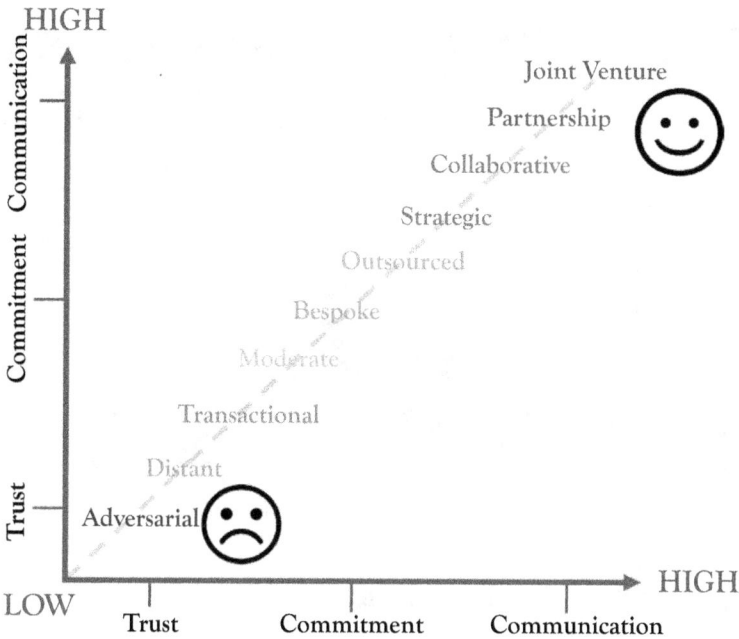

Figure 5.2 Supplier relationships

Having explained the different type of categories of products and supplier relationships, it is also important to explain how suppliers may see procurement professionals or the organizations that they represent.

Just because a procurement professional views a supplier as strategic or highly important, it is not guaranteed that a supplier will have the same opinions.

Figure 5.3 shows how suppliers are likely to form their opinions of which procurement organizations are most important to them. A procurement organization that spends a high amount of money and has a good reputation will be placed as a *valued* customer of a supplier. Opposing this, a procurement organization that spends little money and has a poor reputation will find itself in the *annoying* category, and the supplier is unlikely to want to build a sustainable relationship.

In an ideal relationship, the supplier would value the buyer as much as the buyer values the supplier. This does not always come naturally, and a skilled procurement professional will be able to demonstrate the skills, tools, and techniques to help build a mutually beneficial professional relationship.

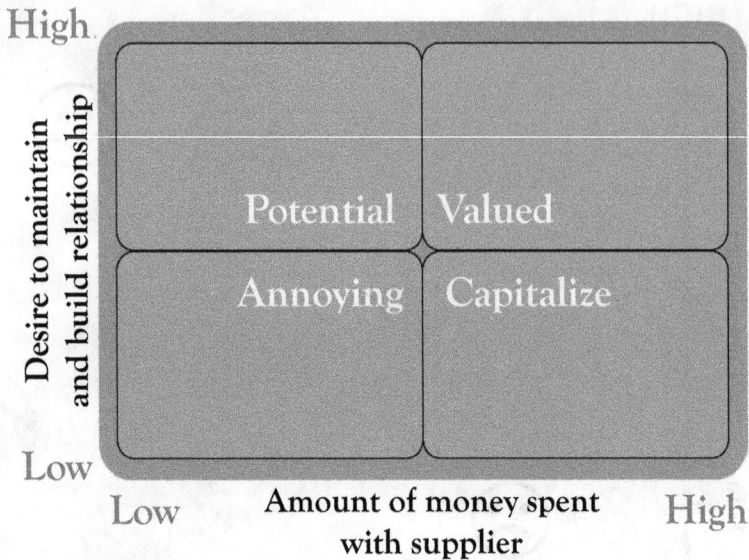

Figure 5.3 Procurement preferencing

When it comes to conducting the evaluation process for a supplier, more focus should be put on the suppliers of bottleneck and strategic items. This is because if these items are not received when needed, in the right quantity and quality, the knock-on effect could be significant.

The evaluation of strategic, collaborative, partnership, and joint venture relationships in readiness for sending out an invitation to tender or a request for quotation should be thorough.

There are a multitude of techniques that can be carried out; the most popular and effective are listed in Table 5.3.

When all the chosen criteria have been evaluated, the results can be collated to provide a logical decision-making process on which the supplier best suits the need of the buying organization.

Not all organizations will have the same criteria for evaluation; in some organizations, quality may be a higher concern than whether the supplier has a good reputation. But, all procurement organizations should, in this day and age, be selecting a supplier that has a good ethical policy, appears to be a sustainable solution for a working relationship, and that is not going to cause unnecessary damage to the environment, both locally or globally through links in the supply chain.

Table 5.3 Evaluation techniques

Evaluation method	Details
Prequalification questionnaire (PQQ)	A survey that is sent to all prospective suppliers to gain an understanding of their business. Questions relating to turnover, profit, years trading, environmental policies, community projects, and numbers of staff may be asked.
Online audit	Some procurement organizations invite potential suppliers to complete an online audit on their website or portal. Similar questions to that of a PQQ will feature, but the benefit on the online audit is that the results can be electronically compared in a faster time than collating hard results from a survey.
Site visit	If possible, a site visit is an ideal method to help to learn about a supplier. Seeing the operations and meeting the employees first hand gives an honest overview of how the business functions.
Employee survey	Not all suppliers would be willing to engage with this, but if possible, asking employees of the supplier to complete a short anonymous survey about the organization can give insightful information.
Product testing/samples	Working cross-functionally with engineering or quality control colleagues by testing products or conducting market research on the perception of products can give useful feedback on suppliers.
Policy review	Any potential supplier that shows a willingness to join the supply chain should be willing to share their policies with the procurement organization. Policies such as corporate social responsibility (CSR), health and safety, and codes of conduct should be readily available for review.
References	Procurement professionals can request references from other companies that have worked with the possible supplier. References can provide good information on how a supplier performs, the timescales to which they work, and any other valid information that is requested.
Financial documentation analysis	By requesting copies of balance sheets, profit and loss accounts, and cash flow documents, a buyer can evaluate how well a prospective supplier is coping financially. It is important to remember that most financial documents are based on a snapshot in time, so these should not be used in isolation when making decisions.

Once the most suitable supplier has been selected, the contract awarded, and accepted, the process of supplier relationship management and contract management must not stop. Refer to Chapter 1 the procurement process model (Figure 1.1), which states that Stage 13 is the management of the contract/supplier.

While the supplier has made it through the evaluation process and proven themselves to be the best fit for a buyer's need, it is not guaranteed that this will always be the case. Relationships need to be nurtured and managed in order for them to grow.

Managing Relationships

A supplier that does not feel valued and does not believe that they fit in the strategic or bottleneck category is unlikely to try their hardest to perform well for an organization. Should this happen, there is the risk of changes happening within the standard of product or service supplied. This could mean that a supplier looks to cut costs within their supply chain and could lead to the use of unethical or unsustainable methods.

Constant review and evaluation are critical. One must not openly appear to not trust the supplier, but should try and work alongside them to ensure that any changes or problems are discussed and any risks mitigated against prior to them becoming a real concern.

Creating and Maintaining Trust

As the relationship evolves, trust will develop, and openness should become a natural way of working. As long as both parties remain open and honest and communicate effectively with each other, there is no reason to suggest that the trust will reduce.

Figure 5.4 shows the key factors in building and maintaining trust in a working relationship. If the majority of these factors, including the centerpiece, trust, are present, a working relationship is likely to be effective, efficient, and sustainable.

Terminating Unsustainable Relationships

If during the buyer/supplier journey, it is established that unethical or unsustainable practices have occurred, then either party is usually within their rights to terminate the contact. The tolerance, or lack of,

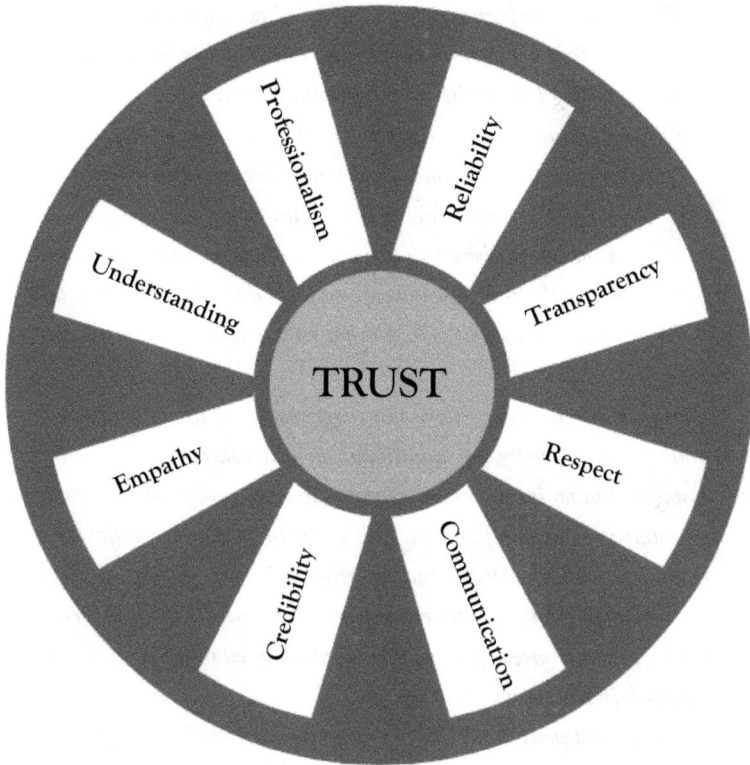

Figure 5.4 Building and maintaining relationship factors

should be written into the express terms of the suppliers' contract to ensure that if unacceptable behavior is discovered, the affected party can remove themselves from their legal obligations.

Express terms are clauses that are agreed between the contracting parties and can cover a variety of areas from price, to quality, to lead times, to warranties, to termination rights. By including an express term that enables a procurement professional to terminate a contract if poor ethical or sustainable conduct is proven, the supplier is much less likely to act in an unacceptable way.

...In early 2015, a letter was sent to a leading fashion designer's senior management from aggrieved ex-employees. The employees shared their correspondence on several social media platforms, and as such, it went viral.

*Thought to have been written by up to 12 ex-employees, the docu-
ment alleged that workers had been, and continued to be, exposed to
excessive working hours with no fair remuneration.*

*Other accusations centered around areas such as the lack of breaks,
a requirement to ask if a toilet break was needed, and permission
being sought to get a drink during long shifts.*

*Within the letter, there was a mention of the fact that if anyone
tried to address the issue, they were instantly dismissed and escorted
off the premises, and worse still, did not receive their last month's pay
check.*

*While the conditions were not suggested to be the worst known
about in the industry, an additional area of concern was that the
managers and senior personnel appeared to be exempt from all regulations and were openly flaunting this by sitting down in comfortable
chairs next to the operatives and enjoying cool drinks during hot days.*

*One large American department store became aware of the letter
and requested a meeting with their contact to establish if there was
any truth in the story.*

*The department store's leading buyer flew out to the factory where
the story had been sent from.*

*During the meeting and subsequent shop floor tour, they witnessed
what they thought to be proof against the details revealed online.*

*Once back in the meeting room, the buyer referred to their contract, which
had an express term stating:*

*"should at any point in the contract duration either party suspect and sub-
sequently witness or prove any unethical or unsustainable conduct outside the
acceptable tolerances of this agreement, the contract can be terminated with
immediate effect or within any reasonable timescale"*

*and advised their contact that the contract would be terminated with one
month's notice. . . . .*

Author's Notes of Experience

*This scenario takes me back to my early days as a junior buyer where I learned
a valuable lesson of why procurement should not be based on price alone. I am*

grateful to say that this story relates to an ex-colleague who will remain name-less and not something that I did—albeit in a strange way, I am pleased I experienced it because it taught me what "not" to do when sourcing from China.

The company for which I was working, made, supplied, and fitted electronic devices for heavy-duty vehicles such as refuse lorries and land-moving equipment. My colleague, who was my mentor, was tasked with resourcing a basic sound system for a well-known brand of heavy plant machinery. The operatives of the machinery spent a long time waiting around, and as such, the plant was often fitted with a simple radio/stereo system to help keep them occupied. My colleague had a sample of the current product and was told that while it was fit for purpose, the price that was being paid from a UK-based supplier was not in keeping with the budget and money needed to be saved. My colleague had some Chinese contacts who manufactured similar items to the stereo sample, so he opted to engage with them. The feedback from China was that the unit would be easy to make based on the drawing that had been faxed over (this was pre-e-mail). The supplier provided a quotation, which offered our company an 80 percent saving. To try and avoid any errors, my colleague asked the supplier to sign an agreement stating that their product would be the same as the drawing—which they duly did. An initial order was placed for 100 stereos for a delivery date of three months' time. After 11 weeks, my colleague received notification from the goods in department that the long-awaited shipment of stereos had arrived. I was asked to go and collect one of the boxes and bring it to the office where my colleague proudly opened it. His smug face suddenly changed to a worried expression and his color drained as he realized his mistake.....albeit the first of two! The stereos did look identical to the drawing and to the ones currently in stores, but were much lighter in weight. This was because they were simply a shell and had no internal work-ings to wire them into a cab. The Chinese supplier has literally copied the drawing, which was a diagram of the outside of the stereo and not provided something that would never be suitable. That was why, the price was so cheap! Embarrassed, my colleague went and explained his error to the procurement manager who, thankfully was very understanding and slightly amused at the error. "No wonder you just saved us 80% of the spend," she said "and at least you only ordered one hundred as the first order."

Two weeks later, the invoice from China arrived, and that pale tone once again presented itself on my colleague's face. The price for the stereos was indeed 80 percent cheaper than the UK supplier, but on top of that was the freight, and air freight at that! as well as insurance to ship the consignment to our office. My colleague was not so quick to go and share that error with our manager. I made my excuses and went for an early lunch break that day and spent some time reflecting over my packed lunch about the importance of always evaluating quotations against their full cost not just the price.

CHAPTER 6

Understanding and Challenging Specifications

Creating, developing, and challenging specifications are key areas within procurement.

Ensuring that specifications are ethical and sustainably compliant is something that is becoming ever important within industry.

Types of Specifications

Specifications can be performance or conformance. Performance specifications are also known as output based, and conformance input based.

When selecting to use a performance specification, the procurement professional will gain higher levels of competition and innovation. Performance specifications allow suppliers to react to the scope of the document and devise their own solutions to meet the need.

When opting to use a conformance specification, there will be lower levels of competition, as the requirement is predetermined, and not open for innovative solutions.

Risk lies with the supplier when using a performance specification, and when using a conformance specification, the risk lies solely with the buying organization.

Table 6.1 demonstrates some of the advantages and disadvantages of performance and conformance specifications.

If a procurement professional decides to use a conformance specification, they can stipulate exactly how their need is to be met and can be stricter in their demand for ethical and sustainable compliance. In using a performance specification to ensure ethical and sustainable compliance is met, considerable detail is required to explain the do's and don'ts.

Table 6.1 Specification advantages and disadvantages

Performance		Conformance	
Advantages	**Disadvantages**	**Advantages**	**Disadvantages**
Access to innovation	Reliant on supplier	No room for misunderstanding	No innovation
Speed to market	Open to interpretation	Standardized product	Minimal competition
Vast competition			Buying organization bears all the risk
Supplier bears all the risk			Costly to prepare
Cheaper to prepare			
Access to expertise			
Access to technology			
Access to specific machinery			

Specification Creation and Generation

When creating and generating specifications, whether they are performance or conformance based, the assurance of a supplier acting in an ethically and sustainably acceptable way is paramount.

Prior to being awarded a specification against which to quote, suppliers should have been pre-evaluated and prequalified. By evaluating the suppliers against ethical and sustainable conduct before issuing the specification, it is assumed that the supplier will act in a manner that is acceptable. However, this cannot be guaranteed, and the specification document in its generation must contain details to keep these suppliers on the right track.

All specifications should contain the same or at least very similar headings, and within these headings, the procurement professional can reiterate the importance of good ethical and sustainable conduct.

Figure 6.1 shows the key characteristics of a specification and clearly outlines the areas that relate to ethical and sustainable expectations.

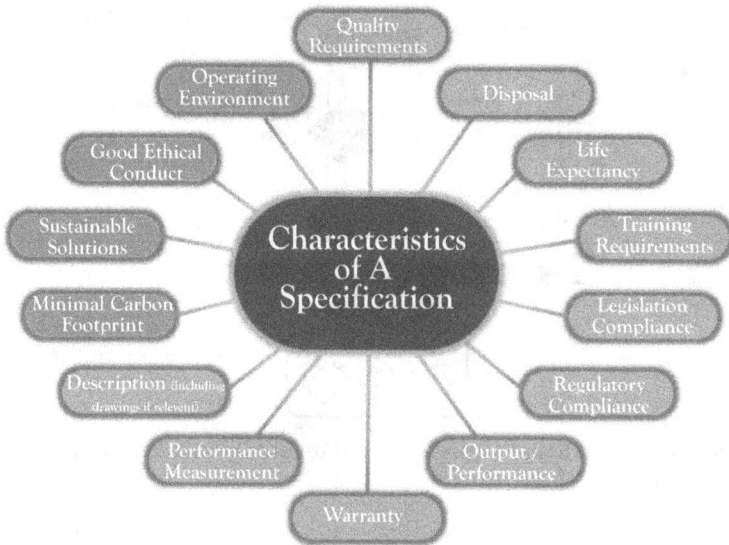

Figure 6.1 Characteristics of a specification

When generating a specification, procurement professionals are expected to have a depth and breadth of knowledge, and as such, it is good practice to create and work within a cross-functional team. In engaging cross-functionally, there is much more knowledge and expertise to combine as part of the process. For example, if a specification is to be created to send out to potential suppliers to provide an organization with an electric motor vehicle, it is unlikely that a procurement professional will have the technical and engineering knowhow needed to create this document alone.

Through liaising with specialists, specific information can be gathered not only on the technical aspects of the product but also on areas such as emissions, disposal, and whole life costing.

Figure 6.2 shows an example of a cross-functional team developing a specification. In the left-hand box, several functions and organizations are represented. To be a cross-functional/cross-organizational team, there is a requirement for individuals from different department and companies to mix and form a new team—this is represented in the right-hand box. In creating the cross-functional/organizational team, additional knowledge, experience, and ethical awareness will be present, which will enhance the process of developing s sustainable specification.

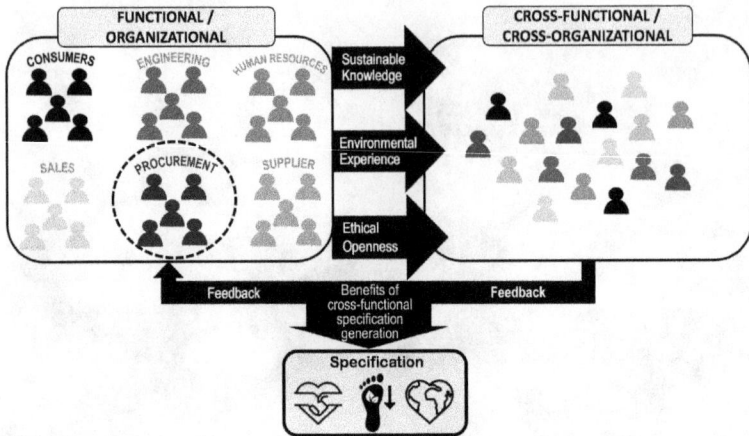

Figure 6.2 Benefits of cross-functional/organizational teams in specification development

Stakeholder Involvement and Engagement

The involvement and inclusion of stakeholders when generating and creating a specification are very important. Stakeholders are any individuals or organizations that have an interest in a business, a project, product, or service.

Stakeholders can be internal or external, and all should be evaluated against their level of interest and power in order to determine which stakeholders should be engaged with when developing a specification.

Figure 6.3 comprises two axes on which stakeholders can be graded. The horizontal axis shows the level of interest a stakeholder has in a project or procurement, and the vertical one demonstrates the power that a stakeholder has. A stakeholder or group of stakeholders that have high levels of interest and high levels of power are placed in the top-right quadrant and referred to as *Manage Closely*.

If stakeholders are identified as having high interest and high levels of power in relation to the end product or service for which the specification is being generated, these individuals or organizations need to be managed closely.

The feedback, perceptions, and opinions of this group of stakeholders are very important in the generation of any documentation. These are

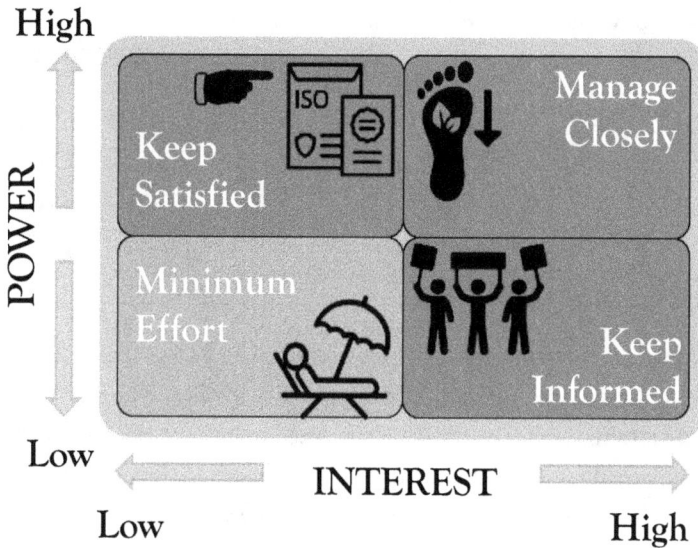

Figure 6.3 Stakeholder categorization

the individuals or organizations that may cause problems, raise legitimate concerns, or even stop funding if sustainable and ethical procurement is not followed.

Identified stakeholders that are rated as having low interest but high power fit in the *Keep Satisfied* quadrant of the model.

These people or organizations have the power to stop a specification coming to fruition, should it not meet the required regulatory or legislative standards.

Stakeholders with high interest and low power equally need to be identified and plotted within the matrix. These individuals or organizations, despite having low power, could cause a problem finalizing a specification or bringing it to market if the product is not acceptable to them in relation to ethical compliance or sustainable procurement. Entries within this quadrant of the model may include local interest groups or individuals who have a keen interest in the environment.

The final quadrant of the model comprises stakeholders with low power and low interest who are likely to be individuals and organizations that require no management at all. These could include people or organizations that have no interest in the product or service that the specification is trying to generate.

Table 6.2 Communication for stakeholders

Sustainable-related stakeholders			
Minimal effort	Keep informed	Keep satisfied	Manage closely
Email	Questionnaire	Workshop	Steering group
Newsletters	Focus groups	Face-to-face meetings	Face-to-face meetings
Once a quarter	At the start, then monthly	Weekly to monthly	Weekly

Once the stakeholders have been identified and categorized, the management of them is of critical importance. Stakeholders who are key players and also those that have high power need to be kept regularly updated with any changes or developments to the specification. It is also important that the high interest, low power stakeholders are regularly updated with developments to ensure that their high level of interest does not cause any problems in relation to bringing the product or service to market.

Table 6.2 suggests the frequency and type of communication that is recommended to manage all stakeholders effectively.

Renewable Inputs

In current times when ethical conduct and sustainable practice are of paramount importance and are in the public eye, specific focus should be given to certain areas when developing and creating specifications.

As most people will be aware, the use of fossil fuels will become unacceptable practice in the near future as *we* work toward creating a world where sustainability is key. Therefore, when generating specifications, areas such as renewable inputs should be thought about and included where possible, instead of using materials such coal, oil, and gas.

Specifications should aim to include renewable energy such as water based or solar and also take in to account how a product is to be disposed of. If possible, a specification should try to encourage the supplier to produce a product or service that will be in use for a long period of time with minimal environmental pollutants and the ability to be recycled or at least reused at the end of its initial lifecycle.

As an example of changing expectations and requirements, the following list states what an environmentally and sustainably conscious consumer would expect in a vehicle.

These types of requirements are a far cry from what has been accepted and expected for the last few decades.

- Lighter weight
- Emission sensors
- LED lights
- Hybrid engines
- Radar alerts
- Air filtration systems
- 20-year life expectancy
- Components parts recyclable
- Eco-friendly disposal at end of life

The responsibility for meeting the ever-changing consumer needs should lie partly with procurement, as this function is expected to have the skills to source products and services to help these *greener* specifications evolve into physical products.

As sustainability becomes an important topic to more and more stakeholders, procurement professionals need to take more time to consider both the inclusion of recycled components and the opportunity to recycle the product or components related to it at the end of the lifecycle. Figure 6.4

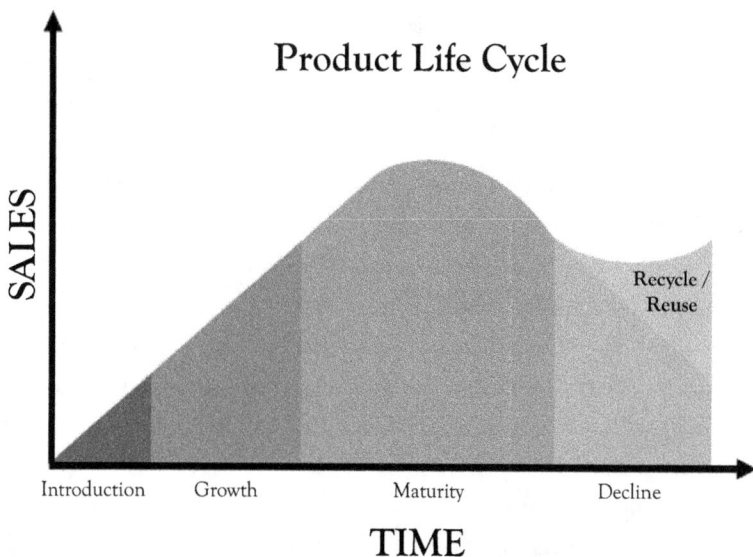

Figure 6.4 Product lifecycle

outlines how, over time, the sales of a product grow from their introduction to a market until a time at which they are no longer desirable and the volume declines. It is at this stage where the benefits from including recyclable components would be seen.

Historically, the use of raw materials has not been challenged within procurement, especially during the time when the function was just *buying*. Now procurement is a strategic and integrative aspect of business, and requirements and specifications should be reviewed and possibly challenged.

Should a product or service require the inclusion of something extracted directly from the earth, historically this would just have been accepted. In today's society, the constant depletion through the extraction of raw materials such as coal, trees, or natural occurring minerals is not seen as good practice.

When a buyer is involved in creating a specification, the raw materials being used should be at the forefront of their mind, and there should not be any concerns surrounding raising issues of the use of raw materials if it appears to be excessive or inappropriate.

Recycling Opportunities

Many specifications can be amended to include more environmentally friendly products such as recycled components or reused materials to avoid the unnecessary depletion of natural resources. Often, the responsibility of ensuring this sustainable practice lies with the procurement function.

While it is important to evaluate and understand the options for recycling for the core product or the service that is being created, procurement professionals must not forget to take in to account areas such as packaging and logistics, as well as any manufacturing processes.

The packaging of a product or associated products related to a service should be included within a specification. Excess packaging should be avoided at all costs, and where possible, recycled and recyclable options should be used.

Packaging does not need to be virgin or completely disposable. Areas for consideration when specifying packaging are listed in Table 6.3.

Table 6.3 Packaging considerations

Specification requirement	Options for consideration
Protective packaging	Does each unit require individual packaging, or could materials be reduced by packaging in bulk?
Products must have polystyrene chips to protect them	Would a recycled cardboard product be acceptable?
Products must be delivered in branded cardboard boxes	Would products be delivered in branded reusable stillages?
The physical product must be seen through a plastic lens on the packaging	Would a picture of the product on the packaging suffice to reduce the amount of plastic used?
Packaging must be from a virgin source	Could packaging be from a recycled source?
Packaging should be easy to dispose of	Could packaging be designed to be reused by the consumer/purchaser?

Sustainability and ethical conduct can also be taken in to account in relation to the logistical aspects of a specification and its development.

The specification documentation should clearly state that areas such as modern slavery, child labor, and unfair working conditions will not be acceptable throughout any points of the process or within any tiers of the supply chain.

It is common for many products to include a variety of components, processes, and procedures, and as such, a supply chain can include many tiers. Well-written specifications by skilled procurement professionals will ensure that any Tier 1 supplier will not accept any ethical misconduct within any tier of their associated upward and downward supply chain.

The same can apply for sustainable good practice whereby the specification document includes details stating that any products or components used within the finished goods meet outlined standards or internal requirements.

In relation to logistics, ethical and sustainable good practices could relate to reduced motion within a warehouse environment, minimal defects and transport only being used when a significant volume has been produced.

Other areas for consideration within logistics that a procurement professional should consider include the viability of using air freight for example, as perhaps rail or sea would suffice and would have a less detrimental effect in relation to pollution.

If a buyer works closely with their cross functional team, discussions can be held in relation to timings, minimum order quantities, and stockholding capabilities to try and reduce the carbon footprint in relation to moving products around a country or the world.

The manufacturing of a product or of products that form part of a service needs to be carefully evaluated prior to completion of a specification document. As discussed earlier in this book, price is not the main driver, and cost should be considered. Cost includes potential damage to the environment through engaging with a supplier that may have a high carbon footprint and may not have a suitable corporate social responsibility policy in place.

Within the specification, the procurement professional should state that any suppliers wishing to provide a quotation or supply a product or service should meet certain criteria. This may include for example a supplier who is aiming to be carbon-neutral within a few years or a supplier who has a high desire to run their operation from renewable energy.

Some global organizations are making significant headway with their attempts to be carbon-neutral. One organization, Unilever, has achieved 100 percent renewable energy usage across many of their global sites. Companies such as this may be a desired partnership for a buying professional's business as part of creating and delivering ethical and sustainable procurement.

Congratulations to Unilever—achieving 100% renewable electricity across five continents means the company is quickly advancing on its RE100 goal as it works to become a 'carbon neutral' company by 2030. Through its membership of RE100, global companies like Unilever are sending a strong demand signal to the few markets where renewables remain harder to access. They want to be able to source renewable electricity locally at an affordable price— and they want to do that now.

Source: www.unilever.com

In some organizations, procurement professionals are not able to be involved in the creation or developmental stage of a specification. While it is the choice of a business that is involved in the specification process, a procurement professional should never be afraid to challenge a specification that appears in their e-mail inbox or on their desk.

Part of being an effective buyer is having the confidence to raise concerns if a specification does not appear to be of optimal sustainable and ethical standards.

For example, if a specification states "produce the plastic widget at the lowest price possible," this should give reason for concern.

Should a procurement professional receive a specification with a statement similar to the aforementioned, it is good practice for the buyer to speak with the owner of the specification and make them aware that by asking for the lowest possible price, the likelihood is that unethical and unsustainable processes will have to be performed. While this may achieve a low price, the associated costs of taking this approach are likely to damage the organization's reputation when stakeholders become aware that the business is buying on price rather than cost.

Figure 6.5 shows what things one should be aware of when reviewing a specification. If the suggestions from the diagram are considered and

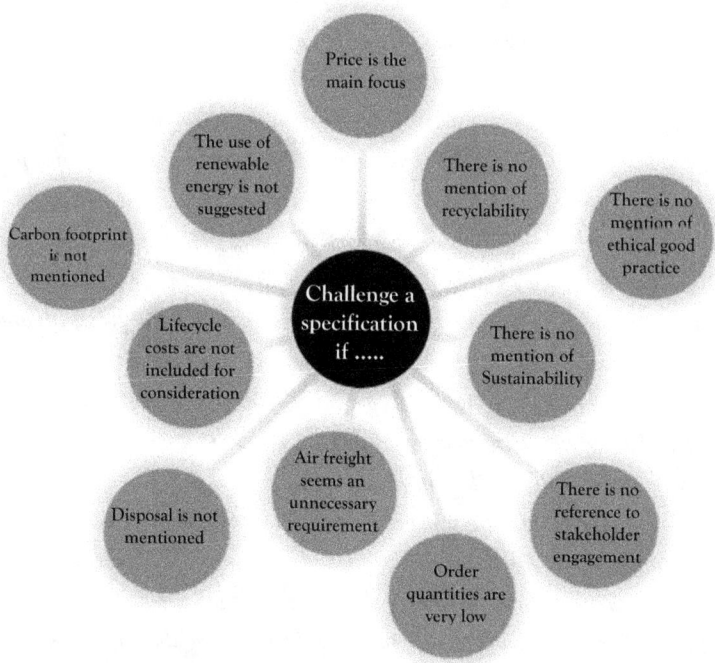

Price is the main focus

The use of renewable energy is not suggested

There is no mention of recyclability

Carbon footprint is not mentioned

There is no mention of ethical good practice

Lifecycle costs are not included for consideration

Challenge a specification if .....

There is no mention of Sustainability

Disposal is not mentioned

Air freight seems an unnecessary requirement

There is no reference to stakeholder engagement

Order quantities are very low

Figure 6.5 Challenge a specification if....

challenged, the final product or service should be as sustainable and ethical as is possible.

To help to ensure the environment is protected and the people within it are kept safe, it is the responsibility of a good procurement professional to challenge anything within both their role and specification development that suggests that good practice is not being followed. By procurement leading the way in the promotion of ethical and sustainable good conduct, this can only give further credibility to the function by continuing to add value within the supply chain.

Author's Notes of Experience

During my time working for a local authority, one of my projects was to outsource the catering function. Our building housed over 200 professionals, the majority of which used the in-house facilities for a warm breakfast on a cold morning or a nice lunch during their hour break. Visitors were not permitted in the staff canteen and were requested to use the neighboring coffee bar. The senior managers had decided that while it was nice to have employed catering staff running the kitchen, it was not adding much to the value of the operation, yet costing a lot of money. Outsourcing was the preferred option, and yours truly was the lady who was tasked to make it happen.

I explored the options, conducted market analysis, and eventually wrote a tender document, which was sent out to the three short-listed potential suppliers. The supplier than won the contract offered best value, was based within the local authority's geographical area, and offered a good selection of hot and cold meals, which they would deliver in each day. The meals would be on a rotation, so every sixth week, the menu would start again. All we as an organization had to do was advise the supplier if there were any specific requirements for the forthcoming week to avoid any risks of allergies occurring. For instance, we did not want to offer peanut butter in the "toast topping" area if there was a new staff member with a nut allergy.

By the time I was in this procurement role, I had a fair few years of experience behind me and knew the importance of engaging with stakeholders prior to agreeing to any menus. As part of the outsourcing process, I sent out a questionnaire to each and every person in the building asking them if they had any allergies and establishing what type of meals would be their preference. With this information, I was able to provide a list for the new suppliers of what ingredients should be avoided or at least clearly marked on any menus, as well as giving the details on what was a popular choice. Some of the information was as expected—most of the staff requested that there were bacon sandwiches available at breakfast time as well as toast and croissants. What did take me by surprise was the fact that there were quite a large amount of vegans in the workforce. Taking into account this was probably about 10 years ago, veganism was not as popular as it is today. Had I not engaged with the stakeholders, it would have been a disaster, and when the staff came for their breakfast or lunch, there may have been no suitable options.

The other big change that I made as part of this project was to work with the human resources (HR) as a stakeholder and ask that they sent out my "menu requirement" form to any new starter. This ensured that (1) I could try and incorporate their favorite dishes into the outsourced supplier's menus when they were reviewed and (2) we were aware of any food intolerances and protect individuals.

CHAPTER 7

Transparency Through the Supply Chain

Supply Chains Explained

A supply chain is a system of organizations, processes, and stakeholders that work together to get a product from its conception through to its consumer.

Within procurement, managing supply chains comprise of working with suppliers to ensure that the product or service is sourced and delivered in an ethical and sustainable manner.

Supply chains maybe simple or complex depending on the product or service for which they have been created. Some supply chains have just one supplier before the buying organization, whereas others may have several.

Supplier Tiering

The supplier at the top of the supply chain, that is, closest to the buying organization, is known as a Tier 1 supplier and subsequent suppliers of Tier 1 supplier are referred to as Tier 2, Tier 3, and so on.

Figure 7.1 shows a simple supply chain starting with the consumer's demand. This has a knock-on effect, which generates a need for the product, and here, the raw materials are sourced, and transported to the supplier who prepares them for the manufacturer. The manufacturer makes the products in bulk, and then, they are transported to a distributor, to the retailer, and finally, to the original consumer who had the need, which generated the demand.

Figure 7.2 again demonstrates supply tiering, as explained in Figure 4.4 in Chapter 4.

Because most products include at least a Tier 1 and a Tier 2 supplier, it is important for procurement professionals to have a full understanding of all suppliers within the chain. It is not always possible for a buyer to

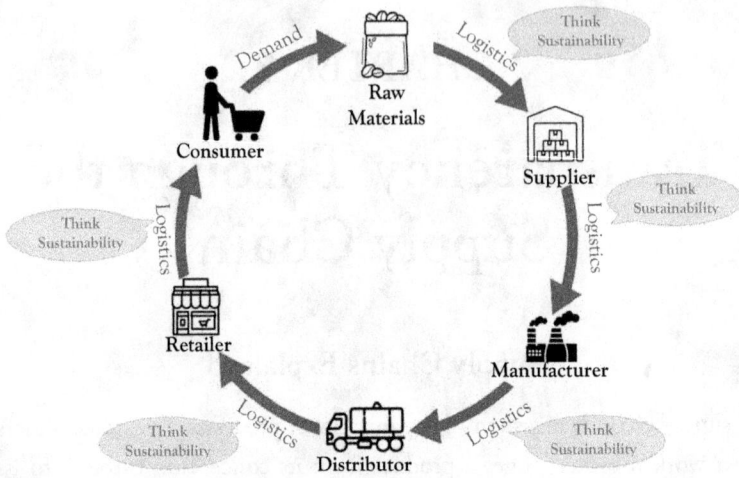

Figure 7.1 Simple supply chain

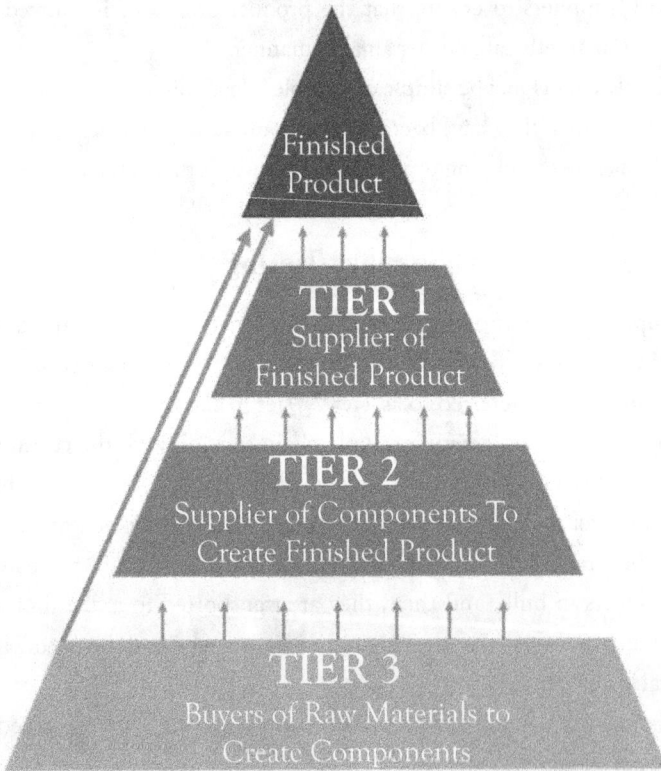

Figure 7.2 Supplier tiering

have a direct relationship with every supplier within the supply chain, as resources simply do not often allow this level of procurement involvement.

In order to assure that the entire supply chain is ethically and sustainably compliant, several areas of due diligence should be conducted by the procurement department.

The buyer will always have the most strategic relationship with the Tier 1 supplier, and it is here where significant difference can be made to ensure suppliers further down the chain are acting in a responsible manner. If it is not possible to engage directly with every supplier within the chain, then the focus must be put on the Tier 1 supplier managing their suppliers, Tier 2 suppliers managing theirs, and so on.

By working collaboratively with a Tier one supplier, it is possible to put processes and systems in place to manage the entire supply chain. The procurement professional can conduct strict due diligence and evaluation on the Tier 1 supplier, and part of this should include reviewing the Tier 1 supplier's policies used to manage their downward suppliers.

It is good procurement practice to always prequalify or pre-evaluate suppliers, and historically, checks have been conducted on areas such as in Table 7.1.

Table 7.1 Prequalification checks

Prequalification check	Details
Capacity	Does the supplier have space and availability to conduct the work?
Commitment	Does the supplier appear to be committed to working with the procurement organization?
Competence	Does the supplier have the relevant skills, machinery, and resource to be able to conduct the work?
Quality	Does the supplier have a process in place to check for quality? That is, do they have ISO9001 accreditation?
Cash	Does the supplier appear to be in a good and stable financial position?
Reputation	Does the supplier have a fair or good reputation within the market or industry?
Communication	Does the supplier understand the language, terminology, and do they respond in an acceptable timeframe and style?

As previously stated, procurement has become a strategic and integrative function within industry, and as such, procurement professionals should now be challenging and testing suppliers and potential suppliers' performance and objectives in relation to environmental, ethical, and sustainable conduct.

In addition to the seven elements in Table 7.1, buyers should now also audit suppliers on areas such as those detailed in Table 7.2.

In the past, it has been acceptable for the whole due diligence process to be conducted as a paper exercise. However, to be confident that ethical and sustainable conduct is being fulfilled, it is good practice for the procurement professional to visit the supplier's site if possible.

By visiting the supplier's site in person, the buyer is able to see first-hand the premises and conditions in which people are expected to work, as well as the environment of the organization.

Procurement professionals should be allowed to chat with the workforce and visit any area of the supplier's organization to ascertain a full and clear view as to how a company conducts itself.

Table 7.2 Audit criteria

Prequalification check	Details
CSR policy	Does the supplier have a corporate social responsibility (CSR) policy?
Renewable energy	Does the supplier generate or use energy from a renewable source?
Emissions	Does the supplier have a policy on reducing emissions?
Pollution	Is the supplier aware of their pollution levels, and are they trying to reduce them?
Carbon footprint	Is the supplier making a concerted effort to try and reduce their carbon footprint?
Local community	Is the supplier involved in any local community projects?
Recycling	Does the supplier have a recycling policy, and is waste managed accordingly to try and promote re usability?
Sustainability	What measures has this supplier taken to try and protect the environment and their business into the future?
Ethical conduct	Does the supplier have an ethical code of conduct?
Ethical conduct down the supply chain	Does the supplier have a policy to manage ethical conduct throughout their supply chain?

There may of course be some restrictions from the supplier's organization, for example, if they are working on a confidential project and do not wish to share trade secrets, some questions to personnel, and some areas of site may be restricted. This should not go against the supplier.

Reasons for concern could be raised while conducting an audit if a procurement professional observes staff that appear to be working in unfavorable conditions, and when the buyer asks to speak with these people, they are refused the opportunity. This could suggest that the workers may not be being treated fairly, and through speaking with them, this could be exposed.

While supplier audits are designed to give as much information as possible, it is always good practice to advise the supplier of the intention to visit rather than just turning up and expecting to be shown around. There is the argument to suggest that if a supplier is given notice, they may change their usual practice or hide unethical behavior during the visit. It would be very unlikely that from the period of time given as notice prior to the audit and the actual audit itself that the supplier would be able to remove any evidence or traces of poor conduct. These concerns are also usually able to be addressed through the requesting of policies, procedures, and by speaking with stakeholders. Figure 7.3 shows what to take into consideration when conducting an ethical audit.

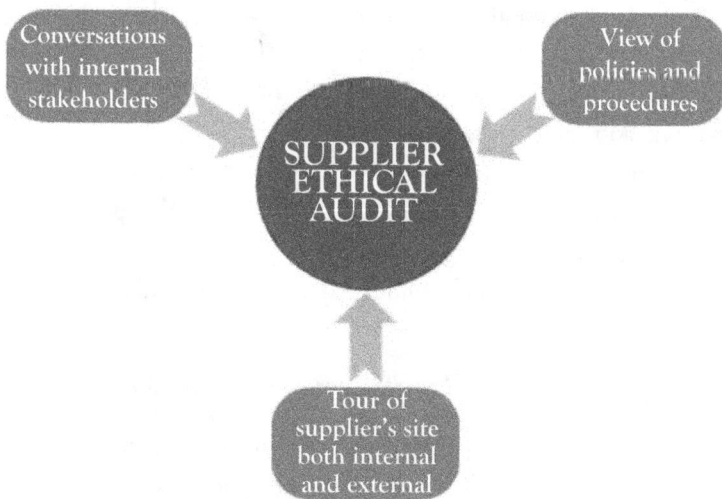

Figure 7.3 Ethical audit considerations

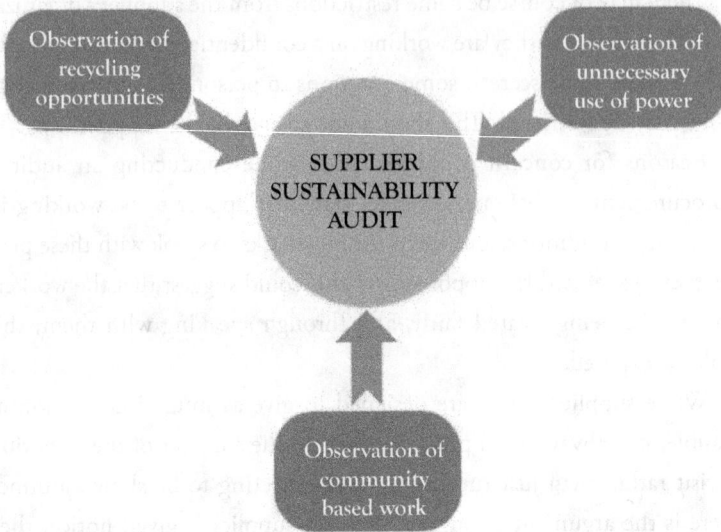

Figure 7.4 Supplier audit observations

In addition to evaluating the conditions in which organizations' staff are working, areas such as recycling, energy consumption, and contribution to the local community can be reviewed.

While in attendance at the supplier's organization, a procurement professional should always observe any lights that are left on unnecessarily or any obvious wastage of power. Other things that a buyer can be aware of during an audit in relation to sustainability include whether an organization has a recycling station, a means of bailing or recycling waste such as plastic and or cardboard, or whether anything that is not required is put in a skip, which goes into landfill.

If the supplier is working closely with the local community, it may be apparent to see through photos displayed throughout the organization to demonstrate sponsorship or good work that has been achieved. Figure 7.4 shows what to look for when conducting a sustainable audit.

Transparency

For a truly collaborative or strategic supplier/buyer relationship to work and for ethical and sustainable procurement to be present, there has to be a strong element of transparency. This demonstration of transparency should first be apparent during the audit process and should continue throughout the relationship between both parties. Suppliers who are consciously and consistently working toward ethical and sustainable procurement will be open with the buyers with whom they work and will also make a concerted effort to promote their good practice throughout the supply chain.

Tier 1 suppliers should be conducting the same process, as outlined in this chapter, with their suppliers, which will be the Tier 2 suppliers to the procurement professional buying the finished product. Tier 2 suppliers should also be conducting the same process with their suppliers, which means that the procurement professionals Tier 3 suppliers are also being managed closely in relation to good practice.

If the entire supply chain follows a strict audit process, there is a much lower risk of unethical and unsustainable behavior occurring. Should this type of behavior become apparent, it is expected that any tier within the supply chain will report it to the tier above until it reaches procurement professional buying the end product or service. This type of openness and good communication is referred to as transparency within the supply chain.

If transparency is present and concerns are raised, there is a higher likelihood of things being rectified in an amicable style. In many cases, especially when Tier 3 or 4 suppliers are involved, these companies are found to be developing countries with slower economies, and often, the intention is not to provide unethical or unsustainable practice and behaviors that are not deemed to be acceptable in the modern world. These issues mainly occur due to lack of education. Through being transparent, the tiers higher up in the chain are able to work with the lower tiers and provide them with details on how things should be conducted in today's society.

Whistleblowing

Of course, in some situations, suppliers are aware that they are acting in an inappropriate and unacceptable manner, and when this occurs, whistleblowing may be required.

Whistleblowing is a process whereby a stakeholder becomes or is aware of something happening within the supply chain that is not deemed to be acceptable.

When a stakeholder has a concern, for example, one employee within an organization may have witnessed several individuals being forced to work in hot and unventilated conditions, they may opt to whistle blow rather than try and address the issue themselves.

Whistleblowing involves the witness of the bad practice notifying someone in authority, and this could be done in person, by e-mail, by telephone, or in the strictest confidence. Much whistleblowing is done in a confidential manner to protect the person revealing the bad practice from any repercussions that could occur.

Many large organizations that are particularly aware of ethical good practice provide their employees and stakeholders with confidential methods by which they can whistle blow, should the need arise. By having these methods in place, the organizations are confident that should any bad practice occur, the stakeholders will not be fearful of making people in authority aware.

Table 7.3 outlines some areas by which stakeholders may opt to use whistleblowing as a means to resolve bad practice.

If all stakeholders within a supply chain are aware of the importance of acting transparently and reporting any suspicions of unethical or unsustainable practice, the procurement function is likely to be one of high trust, honest working, and significant value adding.

Table 7.3 Areas requiring whistleblowing

Reason for whistleblowing	Details
Poor working conditions	Employees may be forced to work in conditions that are too hot, without ventilation and all unclean
Long working hours	Employees may have to work up to 16 hours a day without any breaks
Unfair pay	Employees may receive a very low wage, which is not reflective of their efforts
Incorrect disposal of waste	Waste may be disposed of in waterways or buried
Pollution creation	Manufacturing operations may be generating a higher than acceptable level of pollution whether this be air, noise, or smell
Corruption	Individuals within an organization may be using their power inappropriately for their own gain

Table 7.3 (Continued)

Reason for whistleblowing	Details
Bribery	Stakeholders may be offering gifts or money to suppliers in return for them offering favorable contractual terms
Fraud	People within a business may be deceiving individuals and benefiting financially from them
Embezzlement	Stakeholders that are trusted with organizational funds maybe using some of that money for their own gain
Modern-day slavery	Individuals maybe being held against their will, their passports confiscated, and forced to work in order to survive
Child labor	Children under the legal age by which they can work stop being used in the supply chain

Author's Notes of Experience

Surprisingly, throughout my career, I have only experienced whistleblowing once. This occurred during my time in a large service-based organization, and I should point out before I share my story that upon investigation, the person who was allegedly whistleblowing, was cleared of any wrongdoing.

The organization for which I worked provided a range of services to clients and operated from a central hub. The organization employed approximately six sales people who visited clients and potential clients to book in work or to explain what the business could offer them. The individuals were home based and spent most of their working days on the road traveling to clients or in meetings with them at neutral locations such as motorway services. One August, the sales director took one of my team, a young buyer, out to a meeting to show them how the sales function operated. We thought that this would be a good experience for them and would help them understand negotiation from a different perspective. They would also see firsthand how the services that they sourced were upsold to the customer and consumer.

Midway through the afternoon on the day, the junior buyer was off site with the sales director, I received a call to my work mobile phone. The number displayed was that of the junior buyer, and I answered immediately concerned for their well-being, with it being the first time that they had been away from the office. The young lady on the phone sounded very flustered and was talking quietly. I suggested she took a breath and calmed down, which she did, and then she explained to me the reason for her call. She had witnessed money changing hands between the sales director and the customer and having recently undertaken a training course on fraud and corruption was worried that the sales director may be taking bribes from clients. What I had failed to tell her prior to her departure from the office that morning was that the sales team often take cash deposits to secure their booking of the services, and that the individuals working on the road are fully authorized to do this. The sales team all had a form that they completed each week and submitted to the accounts department along with any cash that they had collected. The junior buyer was quickly reassured that she had not witnessed anything underhand, but I explained to her how proud I was of her ability to understand potential corruption and the fact that she was brave enough to call in and "whistle blow" on what could have been a potentially very serious situation.

CHAPTER 8

Challenging Suppliers to Make a Better Future

As explained in Chapter 7, the conducting of supplier audits is paramount to achieving ethical and sustainable compliance within the supply chain. Audits should be conducted prior to engaging a supplier in a contract and also at regular intervals after the contract has been awarded.

Suppliers need to be aware that good practice is not something that should just be apparent to gain approval on a buying organization's database but something that is to be expected throughout the duration of the agreement and beyond.

Audits should be conducted on at least an annual basis and on any occasions when a procurement professional has reason to believe that something outside the levels of acceptable performance has occurred. An example of an unscheduled audit could relate to an instance of whistleblowing or concerns from any stakeholder that a process or type of behavior being demonstrated is not acceptable.

Scheduled audits are likely to review the supplier's performance, including how they are responding to the key performance indicators set within their contract. Performance measurements and targets will be explained later in Chapter 8.

Supplier Reviews

In addition to supplier audits, it is good practice for a procurement professional to carry out regular supplier reviews. Reviews differ from audits insofar, as during an audit, the buying organization will be checking if the supplier is performing to the expected standards and targets, whereas a review is a more personal meeting, giving the supplier the opportunity to discuss any issues that they may have. Supplier reviews play a key part in strong supplier relationship management.

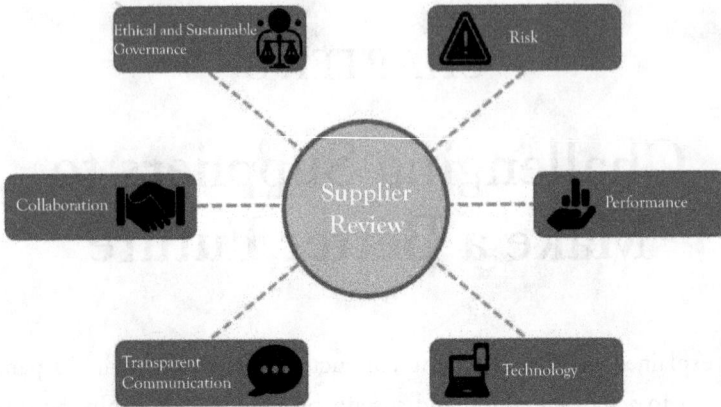

Figure 8.1 Supplier review considerations

By giving a supplier the opportunity to talk with a representative from the buying organization, the supplier has the chance to discuss anything that may be of concern to them. Through raising these concerns as early as possible, the likelihood of resolution is much higher.

Figure 8.1 shows what should be discussed during a supplier review to help gain an understanding of their goals, practices, and standards.

Supplier reviews offer both parties many benefits; some of these are listed in Table 8.1.

Table 8.1 Benefits of supplier reviews

Benefit	Details
Early identification of issues	Any concerns can be raised prior to them becoming significant issues.
Open communication	This promotes transparency throughout the supply chain and enables both parties to speak honestly.
Performance management	Reviews of key performance indicators or service-level agreements can be undertaken to establish how well the supplier is performing in relation to the contract.
Innovation	Areas related to environmental, ethical, and sustainable innovation can be discussed.
Collaboration	Through regular updates, the relationship between the buyer and the supplier will grow and collaboration will develop.
Quality	The quality of products and services will be enhanced due to the regular discussions and sharing of information.
Risk identification and mitigation	Risk registers and matrices can be regularly reviewed by both parties and any problems evaluated and mitigated against.

The effective use of auditing and conducting supplier reviews within the supplier database should start to develop or expand the suppliers' awareness on ethical and sustainable practices.

A supplier may not have all the policies, procedures, and expected behaviors in place at the beginning of a relationship. However, through collaborative working and by the supplier appearing to be willing to change, these positive changes should evolve in a relatively short period of time. Correct use and insertion of key performance indicators and service-level agreements within a contractual agreement will contribute toward these positive changes. More information on key performance indicators and service-level agreements and performance management will feature later in this chapter.

Suppliers' Visions

By closely working with supplier, a procurement professional is able to help them achieve and shape their organization's vision and departmental mission statement.

A mission statement is a concise statement explaining an organization's key goals, objectives, and values. A vision statement is a collection of inspirational sentences, which together form the ideal state in which a department wishes to find itself.

Procurement professionals should be aware of their suppliers' mission and vision statements and be looking to see if these statements contain any reference to ethical and sustainable good practice. An organization that is passionate and dedicated in areas of environmental friendliness, good ethical conduct, and sustainability will undoubtedly incorporate these factors in one or both of their statements.

Not all organizations will have a vision or mission statement, and it is here that procurement can use their experience and skill to help an organization or at least one department within it to develop a statement to work toward helping them to achieve ethical and sustainable conduct and approaches.

When conducting a prequalification evaluation on a potential supplier or reviewing a current supplier, if a buyer discovers a statement such as the following, this would suggest that this supplier has a good ethical and sustainable awareness and is keen to tell the world their intentions:

Develop and manufacture the best product by causing no unnecessary harm to planet or population ensuring that our profit is shared with all stakeholders and invested in sustainable solutions.

While discovering a promising vision or mission statement is a positive step, a procurement professional should always probe the supplier to ensure understanding of how they intend to meet their statement and what processes are in place to validate its effectiveness.

A vision or mission statement that simply exists for the purpose of *having one* is not good practice. It should be possible for suppliers to be held accountable against the statements that they have created.

In years gone by, there have been several occurrences where a supplier has not been conducting business in accordance with their vision statement.

One large high-profile case outlined the importance of adhering to a company's mission statement. The company in question had a mission statement promoting their intention to ensure that the planet was not disadvantaged by their presence, yet through actions in and around 2015, the statement was proven to be unfulfilled. The organization was accused of being involved in unethical work practices whereby employees were reported to have been mistreated, harassed, and forced to doctor their working hours to show that they had been working less hours than they actually did.

The repercussions from the scandal resulted in global media coverage of the story, which generated an increased consumer awareness that perhaps their brand of choice, despite producing a desirable end product, was not operating in accordance with the standards their corporate material suggested they should.

Examples such as this reiterate the importance of conducting regular audits and reviews.

If a selected supplier does not appear to have a vision or mission statement or the ones they do have appear outdated, a procurement professional could work with the supplier or a designated representative to help them create a more suitable or new vision and mission statement. Working with the supplier in a collaborative manner not only develops and improves the relationship but can also educate and encourage this supplier to focus on areas surrounding ethical conduct and sustainability.

Vision / Mission Statement Pointers			
Create long term goals ✓	Be concise ✓	Ensure the statement is achievable ✓	Gain Stake holder buy in ✓
Refer to sustainability ✓	Refer to ethical conduct ✓	Regularly review the statements ✓	Publish these statements for the world to see ✓

Figure 8.2 Vision/mission statement pointers

Another advantage of helping a supplier to create or update their statements is that this promotes alignment throughout the supply chain, which in turn reduces the risk of poor practice or behavior.

Figure 8.2 shows what is expected to be included within a vision or a mission statement and can be used as a guide to help procurement professionals evaluate the credibility of the statements that they come across when reviewing or evaluating suppliers.

Setting and Monitoring of Targets

The setting and monitoring of targets are an important area in relation to understanding how well a supplier is performing. Targets should not be set to try and force a supplier to achieve the unachievable, but should be created to encourage them to improve in a continuous manner.

Key performance indicators and service-level agreements are elements that should be added within the express terms of a contract. Both key performance indicators and service-level agreements should be agreed with the supplier prior to the commencement of the agreement. A procurement professional cannot appraise a supplier on performance methods that have not been included and agreed in a contract.

If key performance indicators and service-level agreements are brought in as a separate document and not referred to within the main contract, these are not legally binding, and the supplier cannot be expected to work in accordance with them.

Key performance indicators and service-level agreements are often used interchangeably. Using the correct format, a service-level agreement is a document that outlines the service expectations of a buyer from a supplier, and within this service-level agreement, is the inclusion of key performance indicators.

Key performance indicators represent the performance levels and standards expected as part of the overriding service-level agreement.

For example, a service-level agreement may state :

Supplier X will always aim to produce products with minimal pollution.

Without a supporting key performance indicator, this statement is subjective and is not able to be measured accurately. By including a key performance indicator such as:

Supplier X supplies all products in reusable cartons.

The performance would be measured in a binary fashion, that is, a yes or no answer.

The ways that key performance indicators and service-level agreements can be measured are shown in Table 8.2.

In order for a buyer to effectively manage, monitor, and control performance, there should be a maximum of six key performance indicators for a supplier to work toward. Key performance indicators should be created to give the maximum clarity in the results that they generate. The *SMART* theory should be referred to when creating any key performance indicator. Figure 8.3 shows the SMART model.

Table 8.2 Key performance indicators and service-level agreement measurements

Measurement	Explanation
Binary	Only one or two options are possible *Yes or no, pass or fail*
Numeric	*A range of measurements are possible* *May be a definite number or percentage* *5/10, 50 percent*
Qualitative/subjective	Opinions about how well the goods are performing or service being delivered *E.g., unacceptable, poor, adequate, good or excellent*

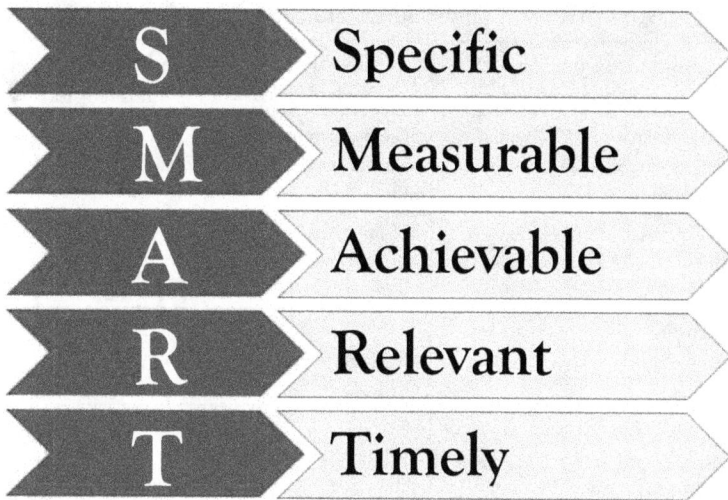

Figure 8.3 SMART

Key performance indicators must be specific if they are to accurately evaluate performance. Key performance indicators must also be achievable. It is pointless and unfair to set a supplier a target, which is no way achievable by them. Should a target be unachievable, the supplier may become unmotivated, and the relationship could suffer. It is important to challenge the supplier, and as previously mentioned, push for improvement, but not in a way that outweighs the supplier's ability. This would be deemed to be unfair and somewhat unethical practice.

The relevance of the targets is also important. Setting a key performance indicator that has no relevance or bearing on the contract, project or relationship will add little or no value.

Finally, the key performance indicators must be timely. This means any target set must have an indication of duration or the completion date. An open-ended target such as *Become more sustainable* is not able to be measured, as there is no time span related to it.

Table 8.3 shows some examples of key performance indicators that have been created taking the SMART model into account:

To be completely transparent and fair, a procurement professional should set similar key performance indicators to all their suppliers if they are to compare the results.

The results on performance are often published in the form of a dashboard, which can be displayed within an organization either in reception

Table 8.3 SMART key performance indicator examples

Example key performance indicator	Area of smart considered	Method of management
Product number ABC123 must contain least 50% recycled plastic by the end of 2021	Specific, measurable, achievable, relevant, timely	Binary
Product number XYZ456 must be manufactured by producing zero emissions by the end of 2025	Specific, measurable, achievable relevant, timely	Binary
All employees must receive training on ethical conduct in March 2021	Specific, measurable, achievable relevant, timely	Binary
The number of defects or rejections received at goods in across all part numbers must reduce by a minimum of 5% month on month from January 2021 until April 2021	Specific, measurable, achievable, relevant, timely	Numeric
Supplier X's energy consumption from nonrenewable sources must reduce by 20% in the next 12 months	Specific, measurable, achievable, relevant, timely	Numeric
Procurement professionals within Supplier Y must conduct at least one audit on all Tier 1 suppliers before the end of June 2021	Specific, measurable, achievable, relevant, timely	Binary

or in the goods department. While it is not good practice to publish suppliers' names and their associated results, suppliers can be anonymized and referred to as Supplier A, Supplier B, and so on.

Should a representative from a current supplier or one from a potential supplier visit the buying organization, they will be able to see that the company takes its suppliers' performance seriously and is geared toward working on continuous improvement. Figure 8.4 shows an example of how key performance indicator results may be displayed.

The results from the targets set should be continuously monitored and included as a point on the agenda during any supplier reviews.

If a target is met or surpassed, the procurement professional should look to replace this with a new target. There will always be areas in which suppliers are able to improve or make a positive impact within the supply chain, and clever usage of key performance indicators will ensure that

	Less than 5% rejects		% reduction in energy consumption		All packaging recycled		All staff trained in good ethical conduct	
	% per month	Target %	% reduction last month	Target %	% defects each month	Target yes	% of staff trained	Target 100%
Supplier 1	10	5	0	10	0	1	5	99
Supplier 2	12	5	25	10	0	1	92	99
Supplier 3	5	5	4	10	1	1	52	99
Supplier 4	2	5	17	10	0	1	65	99

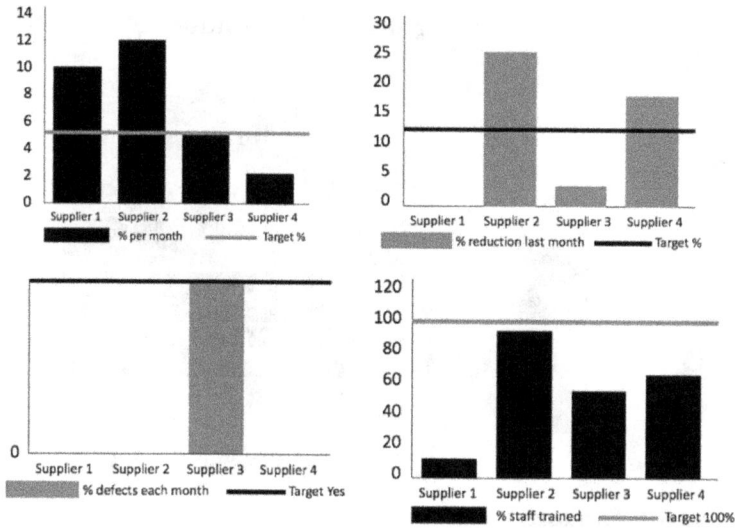

Figure 8.4 Display of key performance indicator results

this improvement is one that carries on throughout the duration of, and perhaps beyond, the contract.

Accountability

Once a contract has come to the end, the lessons learned, the processes followed, and procedures introduced throughout its duration should remain in situ with the supplier, and therefore, through having used key performance indicators to promote ethical, environmental, and sustainable good practice, these behaviors should remain within the organization for the foreseeable future.

Setting and managing targets with a supplier promotes accountability within the supply chain. If a supplier is aware that they are being monitored on their performance, they are much more likely to conduct themselves in a manner that is deemed to be acceptable by the procurement organization. If a Tier 1 supplier is managing themselves in a positive way, they are likely to see the benefits, which are outlined in Figure 8.5, and

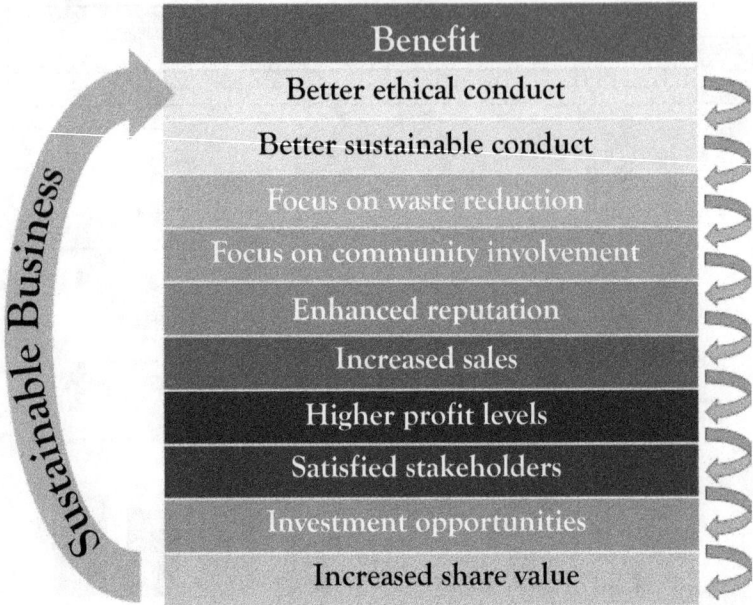

Sustainable Business

Benefit
Better ethical conduct
Better sustainable conduct
Focus on waste reduction
Focus on community involvement
Enhanced reputation
Increased sales
Higher profit levels
Satisfied stakeholders
Investment opportunities
Increased share value

Figure 8.5 Sustainable business benefits

because these benefits are being realized, Tier 2 and Tier 3 suppliers are likely to also follow the same format.

A supplier that performs well against their targets is more likely to gain repeat business from a procurement organization, as well as acquiring new business because of their improved and enhanced good practice, positive behaviors, and strong values.

By becoming a more ethical and sustainable operation, a supplier is not only protecting the future of the planet and the population but also its own future business, its stakeholders, and its reputation.

Author's Notes of Experience

Within the last five years, I really saw firsthand the benefit of conducting supplier reviews. I have always been a bit particular about conducting the annual supplier reviews, even on suppliers that were truly aligned and collaborative. Somebody told me in my early career that regardless of how well a supplier is performing, how well the relationship appears to be going, and how confident they appear, there is nothing as beneficial for gaining peace of mind than conducting regular reviews. That snippet of wisdom has stayed with me for many, many years and proved its validity in the mid-2010s.

A trusted and well-established supplier with whom I had worked for many years provided a tender response to design and built a new bridge in a large city. This supplier's prices were always competitive, but this particular bid was significantly lower than I had expected. While part of a procurement professional is always pleased to receive quotations and bids lower than expected, there is another part that starts to ask "why?" This supplier was coming due for their annual review, so I thought it would be a good time to request a meeting, conduct the relevant audit work, and ensure that everything was well. There was no reason to expect anything negative was going on so, in my head, a regular and now almost routine review was set up.

Once on site at the supplier's head office, the first thing that struck me as a little odd was the significantly lower number of staff than on previous visits. I questioned this and was told that they were having a restructure to make them more cost-effective. Fair enough....

Nothing else during the audit appeared out of the ordinary, and as always, I asked for a copy of the latest accounts and was told that they would be e-mailed to me to be waiting for me by the time I returned to my desk the following morning. The next morning, as promised, the accounts were in my inbox, and I forwarded them to the accounts department to conduct the due diligence. I did not expect the call I received less than three hours later, which categorically told me to "not award" any contracts to this supplier. The accounts had shown that the supplier was in significant debt, and it appeared to the accountant that even if they sold all of their assets, there would not be enough money raised to cover their liabilities. "Maybe that was why their bid was so competitive," I thought, "they are just trying to get as much cash into the business as they can."

Over the next few weeks, many meetings were held between myself and other managers with the supplier, who continuously tried to convince us that the accounts just showed "a blip," and there was no reason for concern. This did not reassure me or the company, and we did not offer them the contract. This was proven to be the right decision when just two months later, the breaking news story on national news was the fact that this supplier had gone into administration, leaving hundreds of their suppliers with unpaid bills and dozens on their customers with incomplete projects. The review that appeared routine from the outside was worth its weight in gold.

CHAPTER 9

Building Strategic Relationships to Promote Innovation

For ethical and sustainable conduct to be a constant within any supply chain, there has to be strong, open, and honest communication.

Open Communication

Communication is the exchange, the imparting or receiving, of information using a variety of methods.

By having communication channels that are effective, the procurement professional is able to both send and receive information to enable them to gain a true insight of what is happening throughout all the tiers of the chain.

Communication can take many forms, the most common of these are listed in Table 9.1.

For communication to be effective, there has to be no distortion. Distortion occurs when the meaning of the original sent message changes prior to it being received by the intended party. This can happen for a number of reasons such as different levels of understanding, varying styles of interpretation, or through a situation such as technological breakdown or interference on a telephone line.

Distortion can significantly affect what is *heard,* and therefore, all attempts to reduce distortion should be made at all times.

Communication that is free from distortion and is open and honest adds significant value to any supply chain and enhances opportunities to maintain both ethical and sustainable conduct throughout.

Table 9.1 Methods of communication

Communication type	Details
Word of mouth	The supply chain personnel communicates directly with each other through speech
Letter	The supply chain team communicates by writing or typing letters and sending them via a postal service or via a courier
E-mail	The supply chain communicates through sending electronic messages via computers, laptops, tablets, or mobile phones
Telephone	The supply chain individuals speak to each other through the use of landline or mobile telephones
Skype	The supply chain of personnel uses technology such as Skype, Teams, or Zoom to hold conversations or meetings whereby they can both see and hear each other
Media	Communication may happen indirectly in the form of a supply chain member reading or viewing some media activity such as an online report, any story on the television, or a newspaper article
Seminars	Information may be conveyed to supply chain personnel by their attendance at a seminar or a networking event
Rumors	Information may be received indirectly from people either in or not related to the supply chain in the form of gossip stemming from potentially incorrect sources

Figure 9.1 outlines the benefits of effective communication when working in procurement.

The Importance of Feedback

An important part of effective communication is the giving and receiving of feedback. As explained earlier in this book, it is not possible for a procurement professional to always be aware of every action of every supplier within every tier of their supply chain. Therefore, entrusting colleagues and associated personnel to share feedback from supply chain activity is an important aspect in the understanding of the supply chains performance.

Feedback can be both positive and negative, but the most important element in association with feedback is that it is honest, accurate, and up to date. When a buyer is aware of exactly what is happening within their supply chain, they are able to take appropriate action, if required,

Figure 9.1 Procurement benefits associated with effective communication

to rectify any concerns, and seek to develop continuous improvement. Continuous improvement will be covered later in this chapter.

In relation to ethical and sustainable procurement, feedback may be received in relation to a number of activities or situations. Table 9.2 details some areas where feedback is very important.

When a procurement professional is able to have developed a truly collaborative relationship with their Tier 1 suppliers, feedback should be forthcoming without any concerns surrounding its accuracy and the meaning for which it is being given. Feedback should be given and received with a view to eradicating unacceptable and poor behavior, not necessarily to apportion blame but to allow education and upskilling of the parties involved to help them improve their activities.

When feedback is shared, it is important for the procurement professional to try and react to the feedback itself rather than look to apportion blame for a company or an individual having conducted themselves in an inappropriate way. Creating or getting involved in a blame culture is not productive. Ultimately, it does not matter who has caused the situation, it

Table 9.2 *Important feedback areas*

Situation/activity	Feedback helps by....
Child Labor	Raising awareness to protect the children and remove them from the supply chain
Modern slavery	Raising awareness to save the individuals from the unacceptable situation
Unacceptable work conditions	Raising awareness to educate the supplier and improve the conditions for the employees
Unfair rates of pay	Raising awareness to ensure individuals receive fair rates of pay
Pollution	Raising awareness to try and reduce the pollution levels and improve processes and procedures through education
Environmental damage	Raising awareness to educate suppliers of the damage they are causing and how things can be done in a more acceptable manner
Unsustainable practices	Raising awareness to help the supplier amend their practices to become more ethical and sustainably acceptable
Quality	Raising awareness of poor quality or defective project which might have a negative effect on customers, consumers, or the environment

is more important to try and find a speedy resolution to protect either the people, the planet, or the profit that is being affected. Figure 9.2 shows how the three Ps of sustainability are all closely related.

Having received feedback in relation to a suspected or actual unethical or unsustainable activity happening within the supply chain, a procurement professional should investigate to ensure the feedback is correct. As previously stated, if the feedback has been generated from a collaborative or strategic partner from within the supply chain, there is little or no reason to suggest that this will not have been given in good faith. However, validating the feedback for oneself should always be undertaken prior to any remedial action being carried out.

Removing a Blame Culture

Regardless of the severity of the issue that has been reported, it is important that the procurement professional does not fall into the trap of apportioning blame. Using blame or being involved in a blame culture is not a

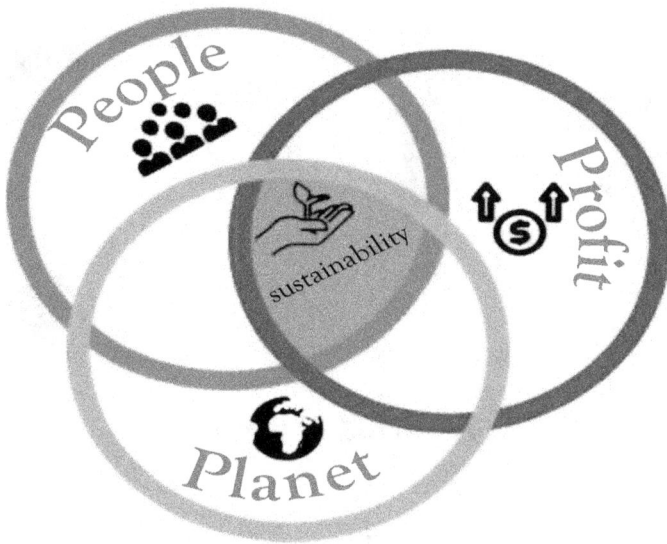

Figure 9.2 The relationship of the three sustainability Ps

productive way in which to resolve issues. Should a procurement professional blame an individual for some form of wrongdoing, the chances are that the individual will be less likely to cooperate, and that the issue will not be resolved or take considerably longer. Figure 9.3 shows two different approaches that can be taken to manage and react to feedback received.

If blame is apportioned, the individual or the organization that have caused the problem will be unlikely to want to work with the upward suppliers in the supply chain to try and resolve the issue. This may be linked to fear, which may in turn drive the individual or organization into not responding or to continue in with the same process but in a discreet way to avoid attention and further blame.

If a procurement professional is able to follow the process as per the left-hand element of Figure 9.4 and manage the situation without apportioning blame, the individual or organization that have caused the reason for concern is more likely to cooperate. Through liaising with the organization and speaking with individuals to impart knowledge and explain the reasons why the process or activity is deemed unacceptable, there is a much higher likelihood that this activity will be improved or ceased. In many situations of poor ethical or sustainable conduct, the reasons

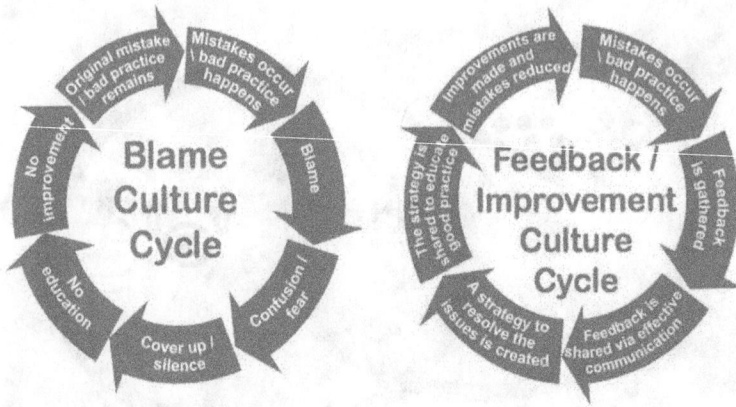

Figure 9.3 Blame culture versus feedback culture

are not due to any intention to do wrong but more related to a lack of education of how things should be done. That is not to say that in some situations, organizations or individuals are intentionally acting in a negative way, but the same approach still applies. By working closely, openly, and fairly with all parties, there is a much higher chance that any poor practices can be improved in an amicable fashion.

Worryingly, in 2020, there were still a large number of professionals who think that unethical or unsustainable behavior is or can be acceptable.

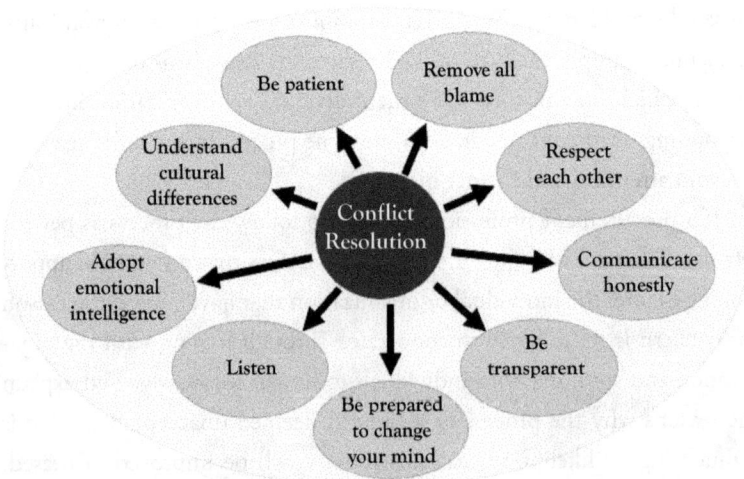

Figure 9.4 Conflict resolution considerations for effective outcomes

Table 9.3 Blame versus accountability

Blame culture	Accountability culture
Focuses on individuals who have made mistakes	Focuses on people being problem solvers
Mistakes are always negative	Mistakes are opportunities to learn and improve
Seeks to understand who made the mistake	Seeks to understand why the mistake happened
Looks to deliver punishment	Aims to find improvements
Pushes individuals to hide problems	Encourages people to raise concerns
Reactive	Proactive
Short-term approach	Long-term/sustainable approach
No desire to innovate	Innovation is crucial

Findings from the World Economic Forum showed that in Europe, the Middle East, Africa, and India "almost half of workers think bribery and corruption are acceptable...." in certain circumstances.

This is why, education by procurement professionals is critical. It is likely that the reasons for which these individuals approach supply chain management in unacceptable ways are related to a lack of understanding and no appreciation of the potential damage when such behaviors can cause.

Instead of looking to blame a person or a business for an action that they have conducted, a procurement professional can consider looking to promote accountability.

While blame relates to potentially punishing the offender, accountability refers to people taking responsibility for the wrongdoing and looking at ways to eliminate or correct their mistakes.

Human beings are always going to make mistakes, but what is important is that procurement work with people to help them learn from the mistakes and continue to conduct themselves in a positive way.

Table 9.3 outlines the difference between blame and accountability.

Effective Conflict Resolution

Regardless of who is thought, shown, or proven to be at fault, the important issue is the resolution of the problem that has occurred.

Conflict is a term that is often used negatively, but it does not have to be so.

Conflict is simply a difference of opinions or views, and this can be used to a procurement professional's advantage to gain innovative solutions to situations or to gain extra knowledge to help with areas such as ethical and sustainable conduct. Figure 9.4 shows some important areas of conflict resolution.

Strong relationships with suppliers result in conflict being resolved in a more amicable fashion. Conflict can be resolved through compromise and collaboration rather than by avoiding the issue, competing to be the *winner*, or apportioning fault with the other party.

Through conflict resolution should come education, which can only be a positive aspect to any individual's development or professional relationship. Managed effectively, conflict can be a positive experience generating new ideas, opportunities, and continuous improvement.

Lean

Various methods and theories can be used by procurement professionals to introduce or enhance improvements within the supply chain specifically related to ethical and sustainable processes.

Lean, Six Sigma, and continuous series add positive changes within a supply chain.

Lean is related to the reduction or removal of waste within any process. Historically, Lean was only used in manufacturing organizations. However, this theory can be very effective with intangible organizations' operations as well.

Within Lean, waste is said to be anything that does not add value to the end product or service.

Waste is categorized into seven areas within the Lean theory. The seven different categories of waste are explained in Table 9.4.

If any process within a supply chain has unnecessary waste within it, the process can be deemed to be less sustainable than optimally possible.

Holding excess stock, for example, suggests that an unnecessarily high use of raw materials has happened, which could mean that substances have been removed from the earth that did not need to be.

Similarly, if an organization is sending out artic lorries that are not full or chartering airlines to send one or two small parcels across the globe,

Table 9.4 The seven wastes (Lean)

Category of waste	Description
Stock	Holding surplus levels of inventory, which ties up valuable cash
Logistics	Arranging unnecessary journeys or using surplus transport
Over-processing	Conducting too many processes that do not add value to a product or service
Waiting	Spending time waiting for something in the supply chain to happen
Motion	The moving around of products or individuals in a manner that does not add value
Overproduction	Making too many products or delivering too many services against demand
Defects	Creating products or services with incorrect components or outputs, leaving customers and consumers dissatisfied

this relates to the waste of logistics. By using transport in an unsustainable manner, excess fuel will be used and pollution generated, which could have been avoided.

If overprocessing occurs, this could relate to an unsustainable option due to the over use of electricity, labor, or money. If an organization is spending money, this could result in a profit not being made, and this could mean that the business has to close.

Waiting within the supply chain could relate to both unsustainable and unethical practices. If an employee has to wait a significant amount of time for a process to complete, for example, it could be that they are being forced to work additional hours per day or week, which results in unacceptable working conditions or low rates of pay.

Unnecessary motion can relate to products moving around a factory for no apparent reason or for people being asked to do journeys that do not add value. The use of unnecessary motion results in additional fuel costs, additional time being spent, and possibly additional pollutants being released into the atmosphere.

Overproduction as a form of waste can mean having to dispose of products that are not required by a consumer. In some situations, this could lead to unnecessary landfill and transport required to take the obsolete product for disposal.

Defects can occur through lack of care, knowledge, or through component parts not meeting the required standards. If a supply chain is functioning correctly in a sustainable and ethical manner, the likelihood of defects occurring is significantly reduced. This is because raw materials will be sourced responsibly, and any concerns of bad practice within any tier in the supply chain will have been fed back and communicated to the procurement professionals. By not using a blame culture, improvements will have been made to eradicate the bad practice.

To help understand if and where any waste is occurring within a supply chain, a procurement professional can conduct a value stream analysis to determine where any potential improvements can be made.

The value stream is the entire amount of processes and activities required from start to finish to generate the finished product or service. By creating a list of these processes and activities and reviewing if value is added at every stage, there is the opportunity to reduce the process and remove activities that do not add value.

Anything within the value stream that does not add value is deemed to be waste, and anything that appears to take longer than an optimum amount of time should be investigated as an area of potential improvement. Figure 9.5 shows a basic value stream analysis, an approach that is conducted to establish which, if any, part of a process does not add value or could be improved.

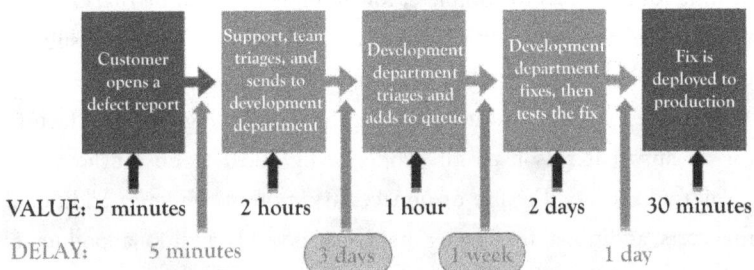

Figure 9.5 Value stream analysis

Six Sigma

Six Sigma is a combined set of techniques that can be used to improve processes. If waste is identified within a value stream or a process is taking a considerable amount of time, six Sigma can be used as a tool to try and improve this situation.

Six Sigma was first used by an American in 1986 to improve the processes within a leading communications organization. The Six Sigma message is centered around five actions. Each process within a supply chain can be:

1. Defined
2. Measured
3. Analyzed
4. Improved
5. Controlled

If a process or action within the supply chain has been identified as nonvalue-adding, Six Sigma can be conducted to establish where improvements can be made. Once the improvements have been introduced, it is important to ensure that these are controlled for continuity.

Firstly, define the area within the process that does not add value, then measure the effectiveness of the process at the current time and analyze the results. Decide on a method by which to improve the process, introduce this improvement, and finally, control the change or Improvement that has been introduced to ensure its effectiveness and consistent approach.

When used together, Lean and Six Sigma are very effective in reducing waste, streamlining processes, and adding value. When considering these theories in relation to ethical and sustainable procurement, the advantages that can be gained by a procurement professional are vast.

In making processes more efficient, it is most likely that less electricity, labor, and resource will be consumed. By reducing these three inputs alone, it should be clear to see that environmental impacts will be reduced because of less electricity being consumed, individuals will not be required to work as hard to achieve the end result, and overall resources will be used in a more effective way. Collectively, these positive outputs relate to a more sustainable future for the organization and its employees.

Continuous Improvement

The final method that can positively contribute toward sustainable procurement is continuous improvement. This theory links closely to Six Sigma and Lean and is based around a continual seeking for improvements within processes and supply chains. Figure 9.6 explains continuous improvement.

Continuous improvement can focus on incremental positive change as well as step change. Whether the improvement is something that can happen relatively quickly or something that may take a period of time is irrelevant as long as the outcome demonstrates a positive change that has improved a process and/or removed waste from the supply chain. Figure 9.7 shows the difference between the styles of change or improvement that may be adopted, but both types end up at the same point, with the main difference being that step happens more rapidly than incremental.

Figure 9.6 Continuous improvement

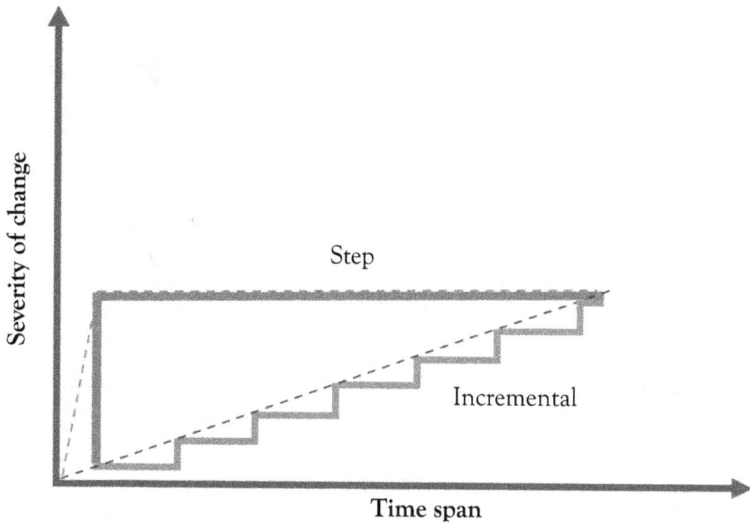

Figure 9.7 Step versus incremental change

Case Study: Lean/Six Sigma

A world-leading center of excellence in science and technology held a large and varied portfolio of international research that supported various technological approaches and relied on the logistics operations to successfully import and export their packages.

The organization was experiencing ongoing and similar problems with their logistical team: consignments were getting lost, damaged, or delayed, and important paperwork was not being completed and stored as required.

The logistics team had started to develop a bad reputation for the organization's customers and other stakeholders who were being affected by the poor service.

A Lean and Six Sigma review on the logistics operation was rolled out to aim to find waste and seek process improvements.

A number of potential improvements were quickly identified. With the support of stakeholders, some quick-change improvements were able to be delivered as well as some longer-term solutions.

Using Lean Six Sigma techniques, the following benefits were realized:

- *Process time improved by 80 percent*
- *Waste such as time, transport, and motion removed*

- *Improved staff retention*
- *Zero consignments lost*
- *On-time delivery of 85 percent of consignments*
- *Improved stakeholder satisfaction*

Upon completion of the project, the operations director stated:

By conducting a LEAN Six Sigma review I am confident that our organization will now continue to develop and remain sustainable into the future. Prior to the review being conducted and the findings implemented I had serious concerns about our profit and the damage that we were causing to the environment through overuse of transport and the pollution that this was causing.

Through challenging and better understanding the way our processes work we are now "waste" free and operating in a much more efficient and effective manner.

I am not naive enough to think that this review will solve all problems that we may face. However, through the skills my team have learned in this process we will regularly conduct reviews, carry out value stream mapping and maintain continual improvement.

For any of the theories written about in this chapter, there has to be a focus on creating and maintaining strategic relationships with both internal and external stakeholders. Transparent process relationships have to be open, honest, and full of trust between suppliers, buyers, consumers, and the workers within the supply chain. If everyone is focused on the same end goal, such as creating an ethical and sustainable supply chain, the results in relation to using Lean, Six Sigma, and continuous improvement methods can only be positive.

Author's Notes of Experience

As part of trying to be more sustainable, one organization that I worked for opted to go paperless and introduce an enterprise resource planning (ERP) system. The organization, and they would say the same, was quite antiquated in its approach and had not moved with the times. Because of this approach, the business realized, maybe thanks to my less than subtle feedback, that things had to change, and they had to change quickly. The amount of paper that was being used and often put into landfill was astounding, and the managing director appreciated that this was not a good way to run a business. Aside from the negative environmental aspect, the business was not able to be completely transparent with its audit trail, as documents were often lost or filed incorrectly. While there was no doubt that an ERP system was going to be introduced, much discussion took place around whether the change should be step or incremental. The senior stakeholders were split in their views, approximately one-third wanted to take things slowly, but the majority were in favor of making the change rapidly. The decision was made that step change was the right approach, purely because of the size of the change that was required to bring the business into the 21st century. It was expected that some of the workforce would be resistant due to the fact that three of them had spent over 40 years working for the company and had always followed the same process. The project manager and the change team, of which I was a member, were tasked with chairing a meeting to tell the workforce of the change. The meeting was challenging, and we faced a lot of negativity, which I feel we handled professionally and calmly by explaining the reasoning behind the decision and using the justification that we needed to be more sustainable as the foundation for our argument.

Six months later, the ERP system went live, and while it was not without some problems, after a few more months, all bar one of the members of staff adapted and accepted the new way of working. Sadly, one member of the procurement team opted to take early retirement due to the change—they were unable to adapt their way of working after 42 years, and I can understand that!

CHAPTER 10

Promoting Ethical and Sustainable Approaches

Throughout this book, focus has been put on procurement professionals conducting themselves in a way that promotes ethical and sustainable good practice. Through demonstrating strong due diligence and being aware of potential issues within the supply chain, procurement will lead by example in the evolution of the function, and its aim to be a forward thinking and environmentally friendly part of any organization.

Lead by Example

Leading by example and setting high standards of how supply chain management should be undertaken must ideally be underpinned by the offering of training to the stakeholders within that chain. By conducting good practice and talking about the way things should be done, it is fair to say that a procurement professional can start to embed the way things should be done in an individual's mind. However, to ensure that these good practices, amended policies, updated procedures, and continuous improvement are all fully understood and adopted within an organization, training should be offered.

Training

Training can be delivered in various forms and does not have to be done in a formal or classroom environment. Figure 10.1 shows the ways in which training can be delivered.

The style of training depends on factors such as the amount of time that an individual has, the cultural environment, and available budget. For example, if a training need was identified for a supplier based on

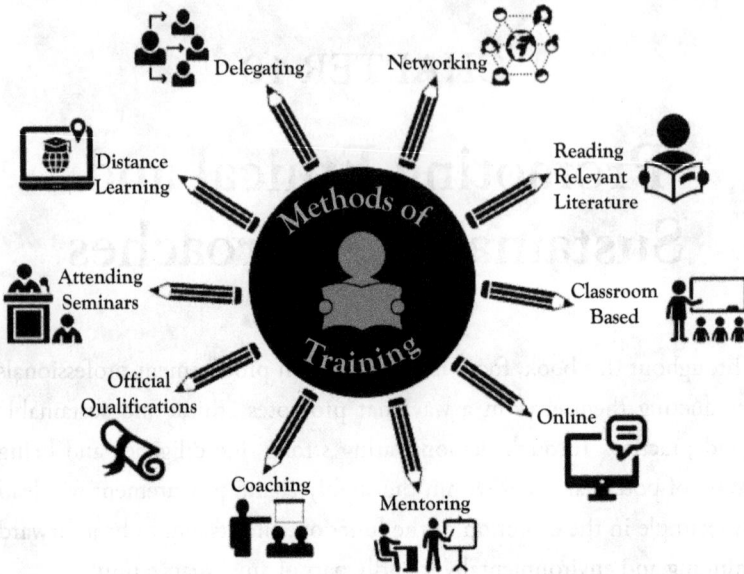

Figure 10.1 Training delivery methods

another continent to upskill them in ethical practices, it would not be appropriate or cost-effective to travel to that country, especially to deliver one, or two days' training. In fact, that would go against everything this book is promoting as good practice due to the fact that unnecessary travel would have to be taken, which would impact on the organization's carbon footprint. In this situation, it would be more acceptable to deliver online training to try and embed the ethical and sustainable practices required within a supply chain.

In some situations when a buying organization is a larger entity, there is an opportunity for an employee that is based overseas to become a mentor for individuals within a supplying organization. This is cost-effective, as the employee from the buying organization is already based in the same country and traveling across the globe would not be necessary. By having a mentor from the buying organization working with individuals from the supplying organization, good practice can be demonstrated through both a classroom and a practical environment. The mentor can explain theories and processes in a face-to-face situation and then watch how these are rolled out within the organization through practical application.

There are of course professional qualifications that can be undertaken to further embed knowledge in relation to good practice, but these often involve significant investment of both time and money. If an organization has the resource to enroll individuals on such courses, this is obviously beneficial, but as procurement professionals, it is important that it is understood that not all organizations are in a financial position to be able to conduct this style of training. This is why, it is imperative that buyers continue to communicate effectively within the supply chain, remain vigilant to any potential problems, and do not engage in a blame culture.

In addition to promoting and offering training to upskill individuals or organizations within the supply chain, a procurement professional must remember to continue to develop themselves and keep abreast of any changes in laws, regulations, or recommended practices. This can be done by regularly reviewing professional publications, attending seminars, and speaking with colleagues and like-minded professionals to share any relevant information.

As a function, it is important that procurement remains aligned and is constantly sharing one message regarding ethical and sustainable procurement.

Benchmarking

In order to promote and maintain good practice procurement professionals can conduct benchmarking as part of their roles.

Benchmarking is the process of comparing one area of a business with that of another organization. The aim of benchmarking is to understand how an organization is performing against the competition. There are four types of benchmarking, and these are shown in Figure 10.2.

As shown in the model, it is imperative to compare processes or procedures with identical or at least similar ones to gain fair feedback.

Considerable ethical and sustainable procurement benchmarking can be undertaken on a variety of processes and procedures, and these are outlined in Table 10.1:

Having undertaken a benchmarking exercise, the procurement professional should then evaluate their findings. Benchmarking is only an effective activity if the results are used in the correct way. Benchmarking is not a process that should be used to apportion blame, but it should be used in a positive way to motivate suppliers to achieve more.

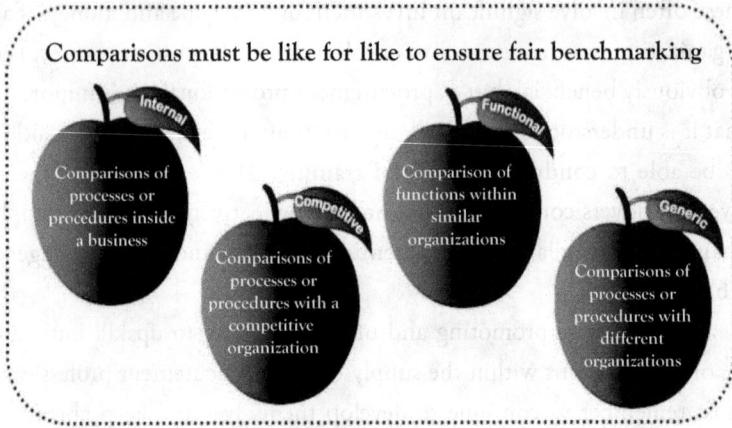

Figure 10.2 *Types of benchmarking*

When a buyer has conducted benchmarking on the selected process or procedure, the results should be compiled to allow trends and potential concerns to be seen.

Table 10.1 *Ethical and sustainable benchmarking*

Process or procedure to be benchmarked	Purpose of benchmarking activity
Percentage of waste reused	Compare suppliers' commitment to recycling
Lean process in place	Compare suppliers' commitment to reducing waste
Whistleblowing hotline available	Compare suppliers' commitment to being informed of bad practice
Staff retention rate	Compare suppliers' ability to retain employees
Hourly rate/salary paid	Compare suppliers' concern for paying staff a fair wage
Cleanliness of working conditions	Compare suppliers' premises to understand commitment to safe working conditions
Percentage of renewable energy consumed	Compare suppliers' commitment to reducing the use of fossil fuel for energy generation
Carbon footprint	Compare official carbon footprint data to understand suppliers' dedication to environmental concerns
Reported bad practice	Compare the amount of reports regarding poor ethical sustainable
CSR policy in place	Compare suppliers' responsibilities for corporate social activity
Supplier audits undertaken	Compare suppliers' processes regarding conducting supply chain audits

Table 10.1 (Continued)

Process or procedure to be benchmarked	Purpose of benchmarking activity
Training provided for supply chain members	Compare suppliers' commitment to upskilling the entire supply chain
Approach to communication	Compare suppliers' approaches to effective communication and managing conflict
Feedback methods	Compare suppliers' methods of gathering, analyzing and responding to feedback
Commitment to continuous improvement	Compare suppliers' commitment to consistently making processes more efficient

Results can be plotted on a scorecard or on a dashboard, which will show the variance between the suppliers that have been compared. The concept of plotting the results and sharing them with all members of the supply chain is to show how high the standard can be and motivate all organizations and individuals to strive to achieve optimum performance.

Suppliers that are performing well in relation to the benchmarking activity will be presented in the color green, suppliers that are performing in an average way against the optimal level will be presented in amber, and suppliers that are showing reason for concern and need to improve to reach the required standard will be presented in red. This way of presenting results is known as a *traffic light system*. Figure 10.3 shows how the results of benchmarking can be presented using a traffic light system.

When referring to Figure 10.3, procurement professionals can see at a glance any areas of potential concern or any suppliers that require training.

Benchmark	Supplier A	Supplier B	Supplier C	Supplier D
Percentage of waste reused	AVERAGE	GOOD	POOR	GOOD
Staff retention rate	POOR	GOOD	POOR	GOOD
Cleanliness of workplace	GOOD	AVERAGE	AVERAGE	POOR
CSR policy	AVERAGE	GOOD	POOR	AVERAGE
Whistleblowing process	POOR	POOR	POOR	POOR

KEY	Poor	Average	Good

Figure 10.3 Benchmarking traffic light system

Using Figure 10.3 as an example, a procurement professional could see that there is a common lack of performance within this supply chain in relation to having a whistleblowing process. Having conducted the benchmarking activities, it becomes apparent that there is an urgent training need in this area.

Similarly, the figure suggests that suppliers would benefit from some guidance and training to try and raise their performance against the others within the chain.

To effectively manage performance and evaluate improvement in relation to a benchmarking activity, buyers can work with suppliers to create key performance indicators directly related to the areas in which improvement is needed.

Making Informed Choices

Making informed choices is something that current professionals should both do and promote.

Informed choices are based on knowledgeable decisions, taking in to account cultural values and exercising an unbiased view. Informed choices should result in the best outcome being achieved for all parties within the supply chain. By implementing the actions resulting from informed choices, a procurement function can lead by example and show stakeholders and members of the supply chain the best way to conduct supply and demand.

As mentioned earlier in this book, buying against price is not good practice, and individuals working within the supply chain should always consider the total cost of ownership. This is one area regarding making informed choices, and others include things such as being aware of ethical behavior, looking to engage with suppliers that offer sustainable solutions, and maintaining high standards in the organization in which a buyer is employed.

Being vigilant of supply chains linked to an organization is indeed commendable, but this should not detract from being aware of what is going on closer to home. Ensuring that all colleagues and stakeholders within a procurement professional's organization are acting ethically, sustainably, and promoting good practice within that working environment and to their colleagues is equally important.

Part of the due diligence required to be undertaken by procurement professionals is to firstly establish if a supplier or potential supplier has a corporate social responsibility (CSR) policy, and if so evaluate, its effectiveness.

CSR (Corporate Social Responsibility) Policies

At the time of printing this book, CSR policies are not a legal or regulatory requirement for organizations, but there is a strong chance that having such a policy will become a requirement in the not too distant future. Therefore, as a professional promoting ethical and sustainable procurement, it is important to make sure that the organization for which a buyer works is leading this concept by example.

A CSR policy is a document created by the company, which aims to guarantee the good ethical conduct and sustainable practices.

This type of policy normally contains three main elements:

1. The environment
2. The local community
3. Ethical good practice

Table 10.2 outlines what subject/s may be included within a CSR policy.

Table 10.2 CSR Inclusions

Subject	Details
Environment	Ways to reduce carbon footprint
	Sustainable approaches to business
	Recycling opportunities and targets
	Opportunities to reuse
	Goals around renewable energy
Local community (social)	Welfare of employees (mental health)
	Cultural awareness
	Promotion of diversity
	Acceptance of various demographics
	Community involvement and engagement
	Charity work for good causes
Ethical good practice	Eradication of modern slavery
	Eradication of child labor
	Promotion of fair working conditions
	Commitment to fair rates of pay

Case Study—CSR Policy Introduction

In late 2006, a well-known franchised coffee shop chain realized that in order to maintain their current customer base and try and increase market share, they had to make some significant changes.

For the last 20 years, the coffee shops had been successful and made a substantial profit allowing them to invest and grow across the continent on which they were based.

During the board meeting in 2006, several stakeholders mentioned that competitors were now offering a more ethical and sustainable service and product to their consumers.

Whereas 30 years ago, very few customers were concerned regarding the traceability of the coffee they were drinking or the supply chain involved in manufacturing the cups out of which they drank, but in 2006, things appeared to be rather different.

From some market research that had been undertaken, it became apparent that this generation of coffee drinkers were happy to pay a higher price, which meant that the products they were consuming were not having a negative effect on the people or the planet.

The generation that was now buying the coffee was one of a very educated background and aware of issues affecting the planet.

One significant action that was agreed in the board meeting was that the coffee chain had to become more ethically aware and promote a more sustainable solution.

The procurement manager was tasked with documenting the full supply chain to ensure that it was ethically favorable, and if she found any aspects within the chain that did not comply with ethical good practice, she was told to "make it right."

In addition to conducting a supply chain analysis and due diligence for the coffee, the procurement manager was also instructed to review the process manufacturing the disposable coffee cups. The brief she was given was to make sure that the coffee cups were made in a sustainable way, and that their disposal was one based around recyclability or reuse. Putting coffee cups into the bin for landfill was no longer going to be acceptable.

The procurement manager was given eight months to make all the changes and told that by the end of 2007, the company would have a robust CSR policy that would be visible to all stakeholders.

The policy that was created and would go live in December 2007 contained the following statements:

"Coffee beans are sourced from sustainable plantations...."

"The workers throughout our global supply chain all receive fair pay, excellent working conditions and the opportunity of education and training."

"Our coffee cups are sourced from sustainable wood supplies and for every 10 cups made we will replant one tree..."

"All of our coffee cups are 100% recyclable"

"We pledge to give 2% of our net profit each year to a charity based in the same town as the coffee shop..."

By the middle of 2007, the procurement manager had conducted an intense supply chain due diligence, visited all key suppliers, and audited all Tier 2 organizations. She requested that any Tier 2 suppliers conducted due diligence on their suppliers. Thankfully, only a few concerns were raised, and these were dealt with through education and training. The procurement manager was grateful that she had always taken a pride in managing her supply chains, as without having conducted work in such a professional and forward-thinking manner, achieving the CSR statements may not have been possible.

Ethical and sustainable procurement has to remain a constant in order to protect the people and the planet. If the individuals responsible for sourcing and supplying the raw materials and components that go into finished products make the relevant changes to promote good practices, ethical good conduct and sustainable solutions should be achievable now and into the future.

Continuity of approach and a keen eye on supply chains must continue to happen to ensure the good work that is being done becomes the norm and the undesirable processes and behaviors that have been tolerated in the past become unacceptable.

Not all suppliers will be accepting of ethical and sustainable procurement and with regret these suppliers, if not open to education, will have to be removed from the supply chain in favor of those who do care about the future of planet earth.

Author's Notes of Experience

Benchmarking has always been important to me and has been something I have used continuously throughout my career. In my early procurement role, back when I was sorting out the stationery cupboard, I benchmarked prices to ensure that the organization received the best options possible. As my career progressed, I benchmarked organizations' policies and practices against the best in the field, I benchmarked innovation, and I benchmarked packaging solutions. Twenty-five years on, I am still at it! Now as a procurement trainer and a representative of the leading procurement global body, I benchmark myself, my prices, my style, and my results regularly. Through benchmarking and recording and comparing the results, I am able to understand how I am performing; where the gaps in my offerings and abilities are; and how my students, delegates, and customers see me. I now employ people within my team, so as part of ensuring my ethical conduct, I benchmark their wages, their working conditions, and the impact that we all have on our local and wider community. As an author, a promoter of procurement, and a practitioner, it is imperative that I am constantly aware of the best practices and behaviors. Through benchmarking, I am able to keep up to date and aim to be at the forefront of the profession, promoting excellent ethical and sustainable behavior to allow me to lead by example to contribute toward the futureproofing of procurement.

Glossary

Word/Term	Description
Added value	Aspects of cost that create positive impacts
Audit	A process to check compliance
Benchmarking	The act of comparing like for like products or services with a view to seek improvements
Biodiversity	The variety of living things
Bribery	The offering or accepting of money or gifts in return for influencing actions
Capacity	The ability to provide a product or service
Carbon footprint	The amount of greenhouse emissions emitted
Child labour	Children engaged in working in a supply chain
Collaboration	Working together to achieve a common goal
Components	Parts that are used to make a finished product
Continuous improvement	The concept of always aiming to do things better
Corruption	The use of power for incorrect outcomes
Cost	The total amount of value needed to procure a product or service including price
Country of origin	The country from which a product originates
Cross-functional	People working together to reach a common goal from different departments or companies
CSR	Corporate Social Responsibility
Culture	The way in which things are done
Cycle time	The time taken to make or provide the product or service
Deforestation	The destruction of trees
Demographics	The statistic study around human beings
Desertification	Unfarmable land due to drought or poor practices
Distortion	The alteration of communication resulting in the delivery being different to the intended
Distributor	A company that received product in bulk and resells them in smaller volumes
Economy	Trade and industry which generates wealth for a country
Embezzlement	Inappropriate use of money entrusted to a person
Ethics	Strong morals and acceptable behaviours

Word/Term	Description
Exchange rate	The amount of money received in return for one currency traded against another
Feedback	Information in relation to performance
Fraud	Deception aimed at receiving personal gain
Globalization	The interconnection of business across the world
Human Rights	Basic rights that every human being is entitled to
INCO terms	International Contracting terms which state when risk and ownership pass from one party to another
Incremental change	Slow, structured change
Innovation	An idea or a concept to improve a process or a product
Inventory	The products stored in a warehouse
ISO	International Standards Organization
KPI	Key Performance Indicator—a method of measurement to gauge performance levels
Lead time	The time between placing a purchase order and the order being delivered
LEAN	The reduction of waste to enhance efficiency
Logistics	The moving of items from one place to another
Market engagement	A process that involves researching the market to understand views and opinions prior to conducting an activity
Mission statement	A concise statement explaining an organisation's key goals, objectives and values.
Modern slavery	People working against their will in poor conditions
Objectives	Targets or goals intended to be achieved
OEM	Original equipment manufacturer
Policy	A document stating what should be done to reach objectives
Pollution	Contaminants in a natural environment
PQQ	Pre qualification questionnaire. A document sent out to potential suppliers to evaluate their compatibility
Price	The amount paid in monetary value for an item
Primary sector	Industry sector which sources raw materials
Private Sector	Economic sector funded by investment
Procedure	A way in which a policy is achieved
Procurement	The process of sourcing and supplying products and services
Product Life Cycle	The journey a product takes from conception to end of life
Public Sector	Economic sector funded by taxes

Word/Term	Description
Purchasing	The process of placing orders and receiving products or services
Qualitative	A measurement based on quality or subjectivity
Quantitative	A measured based on quantity or numeric outcomes
Raw materials	Products that are unprocessed
Recycling	The reuse of products to minimise the use of raw materials
Remuneration	The amount an individual received for work undertaken
Secondary sector	Industry sector which manufactures raw materials into products
Six Sigma	A combined set of techniques which can be used to improve processes.
SLA	Service Level Agreement—a method of measurement to gauge performance levels often including KPIs
SMART	Acronym used to help write KPIs (Specific, Measurable, Achievable, Realistic, Time Bound)
Social aspect	The good done by a company in relation to its stakeholders
Sourcing	The process of locating and selecting suppliers
Specification	A statement explaining what is required
Stakeholder	An individual or organization that has an interest in a project
Step change	Rapid, reactive change
Strategic	Long term, planned and regulated approach
Supply and demand	The amount of products/services available against their associated need from consumers
Supply chain	A system or organisations, processes and people involved in supplying a product or service
Sustainability	The ability to exist consistently and constantly in relation to the environment, the people and the economy
Tertiary sector	Industry sector which provides services
Third Sector	Economic sector funded by donations
Tier	A level in a supply chain
Transactional	Start term, unplanned and unregulated approach
Value stream mapping	A process to understand where value is added and where it is not
Vision statement	A collection of inspirational sentences which together form the ideal state in which a department wishes to find itself.
Warranty/Guarantee	A guarantee of integrity that the product or service is fit for purpose

About the Author

Katie Jarvis-Grove is from England and has been working in procurement for over 25 years. Katie has experience working for private, public, and third sector organizations and has bought primary, secondary, and tertiary goods and services. Her roles have included junior buyer, expeditor, buyer, category manager, procurement manager, consultant, and trainer.

Throughout this 25 years, Katie has seen first-hand how purchasing has evolved into procurement and how ethics and sustainability are finally getting the attention and focus that they need. No longer is price the sole driving factor for procurement professionals when making decisions on which supplier to engage with. This book discusses the ways in which procurement can help to provide an ethical and sustainable approach to business and product creation while raising an awareness of unacceptable practices with a view to their eradication.

You, the reader, will learn more about Katie's honest experiences of working in procurement as you progress through her literary work. At the end of each chapter, Katie has provided a mini case study exploring and explaining some of her purchasing stories that she has collated over the years.

Index

Letters '*f*' and '*t*' after page numbers indicate figure and table, respectively.

OTHER TITLES IN THE SUPPLY AND OPERATIONS MANAGEMENT COLLECTION

Joy M. Field, Boston College, Editor

- *Sustainable Quality* by Joseph Diele
- *Why Quality is Important and How It Applies in Diverse Business and Social Environments, Volume II* by Paul Hayes
- *Why Quality is Important and How It Applies in Diverse Business and Social Environments, Volume I* by Paul Hayes
- *The Cost* by Chris Domanski
- *The Barn Door is Open* by Serge Alfonse
- *Operations Management in China* by Craig Seidelson
- *Logistics Management* by Tan Miller, and Matthew J. Liberatore
- *The Practical Guide to Transforming Your Company* by Daniel Plung, and Connie Krull
- *Leading and Managing Strategic Suppliers* by Richard Moxham
- *Moving the Chains* by Domenico LePore
- *The New Age Urban Transportation Systems, Volume II* by Sundaravalli Narayanaswami
- *The New Age Urban Transportation Systems, Volume I* by Sundaravalli Narayanaswami
- *Optimizing the Supply Chain* by Jay E. Fortenberry
- *Insightful Quality, Second Edition* by Scott W. Culberson

Announcing the Business Expert Press Digital Library

Concise e-books business students need for classroom and research

This book can also be purchased in an e-book collection by your library as

- a one-time purchase,
- that is owned forever,
- allows for simultaneous readers,
- has no restrictions on printing, and
- can be downloaded as PDFs from within the library community.

Our digital library collections are a great solution to beat the rising cost of textbooks. E-books can be loaded into their course management systems or onto students' e-book readers.
The **Business Expert Press** digital libraries are very affordable, with no obligation to buy in future years. For more information, please visit **www.businessexpertpress.com/librarians**. To set up a trial in the United States, please email **sales@businessexpertpress.com**.